An Aztec Book of Days

CELEBRATE NATIVE AMERICA!

An Aztec Book of Days

Five Flower Press

Santa Fe, New Mexico

BY RICHARD BALTHAZAR

ACKNOWLEDGEMENTS
Sincere gratitude to Ernesto Torres for his incisive and insightful editing, to John Cole for his artistry in processing and assembling the illustrations, and to the University of New Mexico Library for access to editions of several Aztec codices.

Front cover illustration:
HUITZILOPOCHTLI
Hummingbird of the South
The Aztec god of war.

Publisher's Cataloging in Publication
(Prepared by Quality Books Inc.)

Balthazar, Richard.
Celebrate native America! : an Aztec book of days / Richard Balthazar.
p.   cm.
Includes bibliographical references and index.
ISBN 0-9632661-1-X

1. Aztec—Calendar. 2. Indians of Mexico—Calendar. 3. Aztecs—Religion and mythology. 4. Indians of Mexico—Religion and mythology. I. Title. II. Title: Aztec book of days.

F1219.76.C35B38 1993   972.018
                                QB193–20421

©1993, Richard Balthazar.
All rights reserved.
Printed in Korea.

Design/Typography: John Cole Graphic Designer, Cerrillos, New Mexico U.S.A.
    Software used to produce this publication: Quark XPress 3.1,
    Adobe Streamline 2.0 and Adobe Illustrator 3.0.
Typeface: Adobe Cochin.

Printed on acid free paper.

To Nezahualcoyotl (Fasting Coyote), poet-king of Texcoco, leader of the Aztec cultural renaissance, and patron of learning and philosophy, whose royal library was burned by Fray Juan de Zumarraga as "devil books."

CONTENTS

Preface ix

Introduction 1

I. The Tonalli—The Aztec Days 2

II. The Thirteen Heavens 7

III. Tonalamatl—A Book of Days 9

    The Calendar Stone 10

    Huitzilopochtli—Hummingbird of the South 12

    The Turquoise Weeks 14

IV. The Aztec Century Count 54

V. The Sixth Sun 55

Epilogue 57

Concordance Tables 59

Sources 67

Index 69

LIST OF COLOR ILLUSTRATIONS

Aztec Calendar Stone 11
Huitzilopochtli 13
Week 1: ONE CROCODILE with Omecihuatl 15
Week 2: ONE JAGUAR with Quetzalcoatl 17
Week 3: ONE DEER with Tepeyollotl 19
Week 4: ONE FLOWER with Huehuecoyotl 21
Week 5: ONE REED with Chalchiuhtlicue 22
Week 6: ONE DEATH with Tecciztecatl 25
Week 7: ONE RAIN with Tlaloc 27
Week 8: ONE GRASS with Mayauel 29
Week 9: ONE SNAKE with Xiuhtecuhtli 31
Week 10: ONE FLINT with Mictlantecuhtli 33
Week 11: ONE MONKEY with Patecatl 35
Week 12: ONE LIZARD with Tezcatlipoca 37
Week 13: ONE EARTHQUAKE with Tlazolteotl ... 39
Week 14: ONE DOG with Xipe Totec 41
Week 15: ONE HOUSE with Itzpapalotl 43
Week 16: ONE VULTURE with Xolotl 45
Week 17: ONE WATER with Chalchiuhtotolin 47
Week 18: ONE WIND with Chantico 49
Week 19: ONE EAGLE with Xochiquetzal 51
Week 20: ONE RABBIT with Xochipilli 53

PREFACE

OF ALL PRE-COLUMBIAN PEOPLES OF THE Americas, the Aztecs of ancient Mexico are generally the most widely known because of the dramatic story of their conquest by Cortés and the discovery of their now famous Calendar Stone.

The destruction of the Aztec society has generally been justified by repugnance for their practice of human sacrifice. Mention the Aztecs and there is an immediate association with "cutting out hearts." The horror of that ritual usually causes all other interest in the Aztec civilization to disappear immediately.

Yet very little is made of the fact that human sacrifice was not unknown among the classical Greeks, as well as the Romans and other peoples of early Europe, and was widespread in the early and biblical Middle East. Indeed it existed in various forms throughout many other "high" civilizations around the world. These human sacrifices were often far more gruesome than the Aztec ceremony—involving ovens, dismemberment, impalement, crucifixion, and colisseums full of wild beasts and bloodthirsty gladiators.

In this modern day human sacrifice continues on an enormous scale—most notably through wars, but also through famine (economic sacrifice) and ethnic cleansing (socio-religious sacrifice). This waste of millions of human lives diminishes all of us.

For the Aztecs, the ritual sacrifice of a human being was the very high price demanded for the good will of their gods and the continuation of their world. Life was increased through the sacred death. Today's child starving in the deserts of Somalia or Muslim facing a firing squad in Bosnia dies for a far meaner purpose.

Viewing the Aztec rites through this cosmological lens, we can begin to move beyond our revulsion at their bloodletting into discovery of the many wonders of their ancient world.* Not the least of these is the Aztec calendar (the gigantic Calendar Stone being only the tip of the iceberg)—a truly magnificent cultural achievement of Native America.

---

* A very thorough account of Aztec life and society can be found in "The Ancient Sun Kingdoms of the Americas" by V. W. von Hagen. (See Sources.)

CELEBRATE NATIVE AMERICA

INTRODUCTION

THE CAPITAL CITY OF THE AZTECS (AD 1325 to 1521) was Tenochtitlan, the Place of the Cactus, now the heart of Mexico City. It was in its time one of the largest urban areas in the world, as is today's megapolis. From Tenochtitlan, the Aztecs' tribute realm reached from Guatemala in the south, far into the mountainous deserts of northern Mexico.

The Aztecs never called themselves Aztecs, but Mexica—the folk of Mexi, a priest-chief from their legendary times. Those legends tell of their original home in Chicomoztoc, the Seven Caves, in a country far to the north called Aztlan, the Place of Whiteness (whence the name Aztec). After a long migration, stopping for years at a time to sow and harvest, the warlike Mexica tribe wandered into the valley of Anahuac in 1168. After many more years of moving or being driven from place to place around the wide valley, they founded their city of Tenochtitlan on a marshy island in Lake Texcoco in 1325.

Thus they became known pejoratively as the Tenochcas (Cacti) to the peoples of the cities of Xochimilco, Texcoco, Chalco, Culhuacan, Azcapotzalco, and Tlacopan which encircled the lakeshore. Many of those populations had some centuries before also migrated into Anahuac from the same Seven Caves. They and the Mexica also spoke closely related languages.

Eventually the entire area was to become known as the Valley of the Mexica, or Mexico. Through the far-ranging journeys of their merchants followed up with direct military actions, the Mexica came to hold as tributaries many great cities whose histories reached back through the Zapotecs and Mixtecs to the mighty Toltecs of Tula (AD 900 to 1100) and the grandeur of Teotihuacan (200 BC to AD 600). From here on, Mexica will refer to the ruling tribe in Tenochtitlan, and Aztec will be the generic term for the period and populations under their rule.

The Aztec subjects generally considered the Mexica to be uncultured barbarians, as indeed they were initially. The Mexica brought only their militaristic culture, particularly Huitzilopochtli, Hummingbird of the South, god of war, and a very regimented, almost spartan lifestyle. These newcomers, however, quickly adapted to and adopted much of the culture of their more sophisticated neighbors. While Huitzilopochtli was firmly in place as chief god of their trading empire, the Mexica also honored the various gods and goddesses of the subject cities. Temples to such gods as Tlaloc, the Rain God, and Tezcatlipoca, the Smoking Mirror, were also raised in Tenochtitlan.

Quite naturally the Mexica also adopted the calendar system in use throughout the subject area. It was of ancient lineage, handed down from Teotihuacan and closely related to that of the Maya of Yucatan and Guatemala (200 BC to AD 900), with roots perhaps even among the Olmec of the Vera Cruz coast (900 BC to 200 BC). What is now known as the Aztec calendar is actually an evolution of the most ancient Meso-American system of timekeeping.

The Aztecs used two very different calendar systems. The first, a 365-day solar calendar, contained 18 months of 20 days, plus five dire days called "nameless" (nemontemi). Directly connected to the seasons, it was utilized primarily for agriculture and guided planting, harvesting, etc.

The second calendar, the sacred "Turquoise Year" of 260 days, was a ritual count used for divination and prophesy. Besides given and earned names, the birth day-name was very important as a person's ceremonial and official name. This day-name was derived from the ritual count of days (tonalpohualli). In it a crowd of deities ruled the days and weeks of the Turquoise Year and strongly influenced individual fate. Indeed the Aztecs considered that one's life was completely controlled by the gods. Thus the sacred Turquoise Year is effectively the ancient Meso-American horoscope.

CELEBRATE NATIVE AMERICA! reconstructs and explains this remarkable ritual calendar. Its format and illustrations are adapted from a few of the surviving Aztec books, primarily the Codices Borbonicus, Borgia, Vaticanus, Nuttall, Fejervary-Mayer, and Magliabecchi.

CELEBRATE NATIVE AMERICA! also explores the complex mythology of the Aztecs' Fifth Sun and the significance of their many unusual gods and goddesses, twenty of whom are directly involved as patron deities in the Turquoise Year.

And CELEBRATE NATIVE AMERICA! retrieves and activates the Aztec Turquoise Year for contemporary use—marking many new occasions for celebrating Native America.

I. **THE TONALLI**—THE AZTEC DAYS

There are 20 Aztec days (tonalli). As in the Gregorian calendar we designate Monday, Tuesday, Wednesday, etc., each of the 20 tonalli is named and the sequence is unchanging:

(1) CROCODILE
(2) WIND
(3) HOUSE
(4) LIZARD
(5) SNAKE
(6) DEATH
(7) DEER
(8) RABBIT
(9) WATER
(10) DOG
(11) MONKEY
(12) GRASS
(13) REED
(14) JAGUAR
(15) EAGLE
(16) VULTURE
(17) EARTHQUAKE
(18) FLINT
(19) RAIN
(20) FLOWER

The Aztec solar calendar is composed of a series of 18 of these 20-day months, followed by five taboo days, the nemontemi. This agricultural year begins on February 2,* the middle day between the winter solstice and the vernal equinox. Each 20-day period thereafter begins with a festival for a deity.

In addition to major deities to be mentioned later, the patrons of these farming months are often spirits of the corn such as Centeotl, the god of the sprouting maize (April 3), and Xilonen, the goddess of the young ears of maize (June 22); as well as spirits of the weather such as Tlaloc, the Rain God (four separate months), and Mixcoatl, the Cloud Serpent (October 20). The seventh month begins on June 2 with a festival of women dedicated to the goddess Uixtocihuatl, the Lady of Salt.

The five nemontemi (January 28 to February 1) end the agricultural year, and during those days everyone fearfully stayed inside to avoid bad luck. Not counting leap days would have caused this solar calendar to slip in relation to the seasons, but it is said that observations of the constellation of the Pleiades were used to adjust it with additional nemontemi. Yet the major cycle of 52 solar years recognized by the Aztecs as equal to 73 of their sacred Turquoise Years does not take leap days into account. The equation also holds only if the ritual count continued through the five dead days of each solar year. In such case, the nemontemi were not in actuality nameless.

The sequence of 20 tonalli defining the agricultural month is also used by the sacred calendar for its ritual count of days in the Turquoise Year. In this divinatory system each of the tonalli has its own special prophetic significance and a patron deity who controls or influences one's life on days of that name. Since the Aztecs sought everywhere for clues as to the intentions of fate, each of the tonalli was also tagged for luck, good, bad, or indifferent. In addition, each was associated with a part of the human body with portent for good or ill on that day. The correspondence of the tonalli to body parts which follows is based on the Codex Vaticanus.

* The Gregorian dates cited here are given by C. A. Burland in "The Gods of Mexico."

Prior to introducing the characteristics of the tonalli, certain rules of pronunciation related to the Aztec language, Nahuatl, must be noted.

1. The stress in a word is always on the second-to-last syllable (penultimate).
2. "X" is pronounced like the English "sh."
3. "Qu" is pronounced like the English "k."
4. "C" is pronounced in various ways:
   a. Before "e" or "i" like the English "s."
   b. Before other vowels like the English "k."
   c. In the combination "ch" as in English.
5. "H" is pronounced with a stronger aspiration than in English.
6. "i" before a vowel is pronounced like the English "y," as in ia = ya, iu = yu, etc.
7. "u" before a vowel is pronounced like the English "w," as in ua = wa, ue = we, etc.

THE TONALLI — THE AZTEC DAYS

THE TONALLI AND THEIR SIGNIFICANCE

CROCODILE
Cipactli

Augury: the Earth Monster which carries the world on its back, defeated by Tezcatlipoca in creation of First Sun; lucky day
Patron: Ometecuhtli, the Lord of Two
Body part: breath/lungs
The day-sign is more complex than usually seen in the codices which often show only the head less a lower jaw lost in the primordial battle with the god.

WIND
Ehecatl

Augury: secrets, mystery, breath of life, flow of intelligence, pleasure and suffering, spiritual life; neutral as to luck
Patron: Quetzalcoatl, the Plumed Serpent
Body part: liver
The day-sign Ehecatl, God of the Wind, is a manifestation of Quetzalcoatl always shown with a strange beak. The illustration is based on the Calendar Stone.

HOUSE
Calli

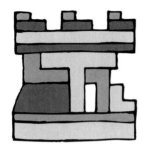

Augury: nobility, intelligence; lucky day
Patron: Tepeyollotl, Heart of the Mountain
Body part: right eye
The illustration is based on the Calendar Stone and represents a temple-house (teocalli). The centers in which Aztec boys were educated in battle skills and culture were called telpochcalli; for the priesthood, calmecac.

LIZARD
Cuetzpallin

Augury: symbol of sex; neutral as to luck
Patron: Huehuecoyotl, the Old Coyote
Body part: womb, female genitalia
The illustration is based on the Calendar Stone.

SNAKE
Coatl

Augury: mystical power; lucky day
Patron: Chalchiuhtlicue, the Jade Skirt
Body part: male genitalia
The illustration is from a design on an artifact known as the Montezuma Box.

DEATH
Miquitzli

Augury: penitential offerings; neutral as to luck
Patron: Tecciztecatl, God of the Moon
Body part: forehead (skull)
The skull features frequently in Aztec art. Its significance was far less morbid than the modern connotations of death, poison, and piracy. The image continues to be central to the contemporary Mexican Day of the Dead (Día de los Muertos) celebrations. The crown of this skull is adorned with a mystical symbol known as "burning water."

DEER
Mazatl

Augury: timidity; lucky day
Patron: Tlaloc, the Rain God
Body part: right leg

RABBIT
Tochtli

Augury: tricky, day of divination, penitential offerings; unlucky day
Patron: Mayauel, Goddess of Pulque
Body part: left ear
The rabbit is also the symbol of drunkenness. The many deities of drunkenness are known as the "400 rabbits." Four hundred, or 20 times 20, is the generic Aztec term for a huge number.

THE TONALLI — THE AZTEC DAYS

WATER
Atl

Augury: passage through life; lucky day
Patron: Xiuhtecuhtli, Lord of the Turquoise
Body part: back of head, hair

MONKEY
Ozomatli

Augury: erotic, emotional, immoral, riches or war; neutral as to luck
Patron: Xochipilli, Prince of Flowers
Body part: left arm
The illustration is based on Codex Vaticanus.

REED
Acatl

Augury: lucky day
Patron: Tezcatlipoca, the Smoking Mirror
Body part: heart
The reed was used for making war darts and arrows.

DOG
Itzcuintli

Augury: companion of the soul in Mictlan, the Land of the Dead; the dog then passes through the fire back into life; neutral as to luck
Patron: Mictlantecuhtli, Lord of the Land of the Dead
Body part: nose

GRASS
Malinalli

Augury: penance, self-flagellation, offering sorrow and pain to gods; unlucky day
Patron: Patecatl, God of Medicine
Body part: bowels

JAGUAR
Ocelotl

Augury: bravery, patron of scouts, vicious in business; lucky day
Patron: Tlazolteotl, the Goddess of Filth
Body part: left leg
The illustration is based on the Calendar Stone.

EAGLE
Cuauhtli

Augury: bravery, watches over world from above, day of sacrificing for a new life, renewal; neutral as to luck
Patron: Xipe Totec, the Flayed God
Body part: right arm
The illustration is based on Codex Vaticanus.

EARTHQUAKE
Ollin

Augury: sacred day of prayer; unlucky day
Patron: Xolotl, the Evening Star
Body part: tongue
The illustration, the face of the god Tonatiuh, is based on the Calendar Stone. The day-sign is more frequently shown as a much simpler lobed form. The word Ollin is sometimes translated as "movement."

RAIN
Quiahuitl

Augury: quiet plenty, peaceful; lucky day
Patron: Chantico, Goddess of the Hearth
Body part: left eye
The illustration, one of the many lesser tlalocs or rain gods, is based on the Calendar Stone.

VULTURE
Cozcacuauhtli

Augury: symbol of riches; lucky day
Patron: Itzpapalotl, the Obsidian Butterfly
Body part: right ear
The illustration is mostly from Codex Borgia.

FLINT
Tecpatl

Augury: great riches, pride; both lucky and unlucky day
Patron: Chalchiuhtotolin, the Jade Turkey
Body part: teeth
The day-sign is the sacrificial knife.

FLOWER
Xochitl

Augury: symbol of soul, evanescent, music and dance, free of sin, essential holiness; neutral as to luck
Patron: Xochiquetzal, the Flower Feather
Body part: breast, chest
Xochitl is frequent in female names.

II.

THE THIRTEEN HEAVENS

CONTAINING ONLY 260 DAYS, THE AZTEC Turquoise Year is shorter than the solar year. It is a cyclical 13-count through the basic progression of the 20 tonalli. The ritual count of days (tonalpohualli) starts One Crocodile, Two Wind, Three House through Thirteen Reed, continues One Jaguar, Two Eagle... and Seven Flower, Eight Crocodile... and ends after 20 cycles with Thirteen Flower. The next day is then again One Crocodile, beginning another Turquoise Year.

The Turquoise Year thus contains 20 weeks of 13 differently numbered tonalli. The number 13, which was thought by the Aztecs to be very lucky, symbolizes their Thirteen Heavens. The mythical qualities of most of the heavens, unfortunately, can only be inferred from the patron deity of each number. These again are characterized as lucky, unlucky, or neutral as to luck and may bear additional auguries.

The Aztec numerals "one" to "thirteen" used in the Turquoise Year are written as the corresponding number of dots. The ancient codices group them in several ways, including stacks, strings by fives, or even scattered around the day-sign. All styles require the reader to count through each number, especially tedious with larger numbers. In this Book of Days the groupings of dots for each number are arranged in specific shapes which can also serve as the numeral.

ONE
ce

Augury: the beginning; lucky number
Patron: Xiuhtecuhtli, Lord of the Turquoise

TWO
ome

Augury: duality, union of opposites; neutral as to luck
Patron: Omecihuatl, the Lady of Two, the supreme ruler of all the Thirteen Heavens

THREE
yeyi

Augury: unlucky number
Patron: Chalchiuhtlicue, the Jade Skirt

FOUR
nahui

Augury: the four directions, sacred; lucky number
Patron: Tonatiuh, the Fifth Sun, whose fourth heaven is reserved for dead warriors

FIVE
macuilli

Augury: the center, precious stones; lucky number
Patron: Tlazolteotl, Goddess of Filth

SIX
chicuacen (five and one)

Augury: neutral as to luck
Patron: Xochiquetzal, the Flower Feather

SEVEN
chicome (five and two)

Augury: completion, universality; lucky number
Patron: Xochipilli, the Prince of Flowers

EIGHT
chicueyi (five and three)

Augury: the eight hills departed souls must cross to Mictlan, the Land of the Dead; neutral as to luck
Patron: Tlaloc, the Rain God. His eighth heaven, full of rainbows, flowers, and butterflies, awaits victims of drowning or certain diseases.

NINE
chicnahui (five and four)

Augury: the nine rivers departed souls must cross to Mictlan; very unlucky number
Patron: Quetzalcoatl, the Plumed Serpent
The Aztecs considered there to be nine hours of the night.

TEN
mahtlactli

Augury: unlucky number
Patron: Tezcatlipoca, the Smoking Mirror

ELEVEN
mahtlactli ihuan ce (ten and one)

Augury: neutral as to luck
Patron: Huehueteotl, the Old God

TWELVE
mahtlactli ihuan ome (ten and two)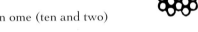

Augury: unlucky number
Patron: Ehecatl, the God of Wind

THIRTEEN
mahtlactli ihuan yeyi (ten and three)

Augury: very lucky number
Patron: Itzpapalotl, the Obsidian Butterfly
The Aztecs counted 13 daytime hours. The significance of the number may also derive from the fact that there are 13 moons in the solar year and 13 days in each of their waxings and wanings.

IV.
TONALAMATL — A BOOK OF DAYS

TONALAMATL IS A COMPOUND OF THE Nahuatl words tonalli, the days, and amatl, paper.

The Aztecs made a true paper from bark fiber that was widely available through the the public markets. It was much used for ceremonial ornamentation, a practice still prevalent in modern Mexico. In addition, as exemplified by the surviving codices, long strips of paper, the surfaces often burnished for writing or painting, were folded into books. These were "written" in a pictorial language not unlike hieroglyphics. They were generally colorful and beautiful, if at times frightening in details, in styles expressive of different regions and scribal artists. Several tonalamatls have survived. There are also histories, particularly of the Mixtec, instructional works, and legends. They are fascinating glimpses of what once existed.

In burning the many Aztec libraries and archives in Mexico and the Mayan Yucatan, the Spanish clergy destroyed virtually the entire recorded knowledge of ancient Native America. The burning of the Aztec "devil books" rivals in infamy that of the Library of Alexandria.

May this new Tonalamatl evoke the exotic beauty of ancient Aztec art and culture, as though it were a small codex that somehow has miraculously escaped the conflagration.

Ancient examples of the tonalamatl such as the beautiful Codex Borbonicus often depict the 20 weeks in richly complex formats. Aztec scribes filled spaces with additional symbols of offerings, etc., and further complicated each day with its particular bird association (of importance for omens) or the contrasting deities of day and night hours. For clarity this Tonalamatl presents only the ritual tonalpohualli and the patron deity of each week.

Each of the 20 13-day weeks of the sacred Turquoise Year is ruled by a specific deity who influences fate during that time. Details of which deity is associated with which week vary slightly among sources. The following correspondence is again taken from C. A. Burland in "The Gods of Mexico," with occasional license as noted.

While there are few clear divisions between the many Aztec gods and goddesses according to traditional western notions of good and evil, the Aztecs did mythologize titanic struggles between those opposing forces for the soul of man. Each deity has light and dark sides and is capable of benefit or ill for the Aztec mortal. A wide and often overlapping range of characteristics makes the divine seem peculiarly human.

THE CALENDAR STONE

The Aztec Calendar Stone, on display at the Museo Nacional in Mexico City, is a fitting image to begin any work on the Aztec calendar. Known as the Stone of the Suns, this monumental work of art is a stone disk 12 feet across and weighing 24 tons. The intricate design on its face has far more to do with mythology than with actual calendar reckoning. The Stone is in truth a highly complex hieroglyph of the entire Aztec cosmology.

The central face on the Stone, within the green circle, is that of the god Tonatiuh, the primordial creative deity. He is the god who cast himself into the flames and was resurrected. He is the giver of all, but demands sacrifice (note sacrificial knife as tongue). He is also a patron of warriors. The red figure with four red-centered dots containing the divine face is the day-sign Four Earthquake. This was the name given by the Aztecs to their world and time, the Fifth Sun.

Within the four lobes of that day-sign are the names of the preceding four Suns (counting from upper right counterclockwise): Four Jaguar, the First Sun, ruled by Tezcatlipoca, destroyed by jaguars; Four Wind, the Second Sun, ruled by Quetzalcoatl, destroyed by wind; Four Rain, the Third Sun, ruled by Tlaloc, destroyed by rain; and Four Water, the Fourth Sun, ruled by Chalchiuhtlicue, destroyed by water. The pattern suggests that the Fifth Sun was destined to be destroyed by earthquake.

The various day-signs squeezed in above and below the central Four Earthquake (One Flint, Seven Monkey, etc.) and the day or year Thirteen Reed at the top of the whole design may be names of rulers or dates of the creation of the Stone of the Suns (known to be 1479-81).

Outside the blue circle, within the red, the 20 tonalli occur again in counterclockwise order from the top. They are surrounded by intricate decorative elements which complete the radiant disk of the Fifth Sun.

Encompassing the hieroglyph of the Fifth Sun are two Fire Serpents (Xiuhcoatl), emblems of the sacred Turquoise Year. In their mouths are the faces of two gods, probably Xiuhtecuhtli, ruler of time, and possibly Quetzalcoatl, who brought mankind the ritual calendar.

IV. TONALAMATL — A BOOK OF DAYS

HUITZILOPOCHTLI
—HUMMINGBIRD OF THE SOUTH

Recognizing the dominance of the Mexica in the Aztec world, a politically proper prelude to this new Aztec Tonalamatl is to present the chief god of their pantheon, Huitzilopochtli, Hummingbird of the South. Otherwise, he plays no role in the sacred calendar which was being counted long before his arrival in the Valley of Mexico.

Huitzilopochtli is the god of war, force, power, action, accomplishment, and nobility. Lord of warriors of the day, the Eagle knights, and wielder of the Fire Serpent, he is sometimes called the blue Tezcatlipoca, the sun at midday. The Mexica promoted him over Ometecuhtli as god of the South. His birth day-name is One Flint.

Huitzilopochtli apparently was a legendary leader of the Mexica clan who was deified. The Spanish reported that his idol was a piece of dried wood carried in a coffer of reeds. In the evolving mythology, his family was also eventually promoted to divinity.

Coatlicue, the Snake Skirt, is a minor earth goddess appropriated for the function of mother of Huitzilopochtli. In the legend she is sweeping the temple grounds when a ball of feathers falls at her feet. Putting it to her bosom, she conceives. Her many sons are angered by her pregnancy and so determine to kill her, but the child leaps forth brandishing the Fire Serpent and slays all his brothers. Coatlicue was given some functions of Tlazolteotl and Tonantzin by the Mexica, and she became a goddess of agriculture, fertility, and rain. She is also believed to be the Earth Monster Cipactli and can bring famine.

Coyolxauhqui, the Golden Bells, is a sister of Huitzilopochtli. Because she opposed his will, the god cut out her heart and dismembered her, turning her head into the moon. She is the goddess of greed and ambition, discontinuity and dissolution, and rebellion. The Mexica promoted her over the ancient male god of the moon, Tecciztecatl.

In the migration legend another sister of Huitzilopochtli, Malinalxochitl, Grass Flower, was a great sorceress. In another internecine power struggle the god bade the Mexica to abandon her en route, and there she founded the city of Malinalco. Years later her son Copil set out to take vengeance on his uncle but was captured by the Mexica. His heart was thrown out into the middle of the lake, and from it there grew a giant cactus upon which an eagle sat—the prophetic place the Mexica were to seek as their home promised by the god, the Place of the Cactus, Tenochtitlan.

IV. TONALAMATL – A BOOK OF DAYS

WEEK ONE

ONE CROCODILE

Augury: those born in this period will be happy; lucky week

Patron: Ometecuhtli and Omecihuatl, Lord and Lady of Two. Parents of all other gods, they exist in a creative pair. As creator gods, they are also known as Tonacatecuhtli and Tonacacihuatl, Lord and Lady of Everything, creators of the legendary Earth Monster Cipactli. With the other names of Ilamatecuhtli and Ilamacihuatl their festival begins the seventeenth agricultural month. The divine pair is the patron of the South.

Ometecuhtli represents instinctual and sexual life and, more broadly, the unity of opposing factors. He exists outside the universe, shunning temples and ceremonies. As the male creative force, he may also manifest in Tlaltecuhtli, Lord of the Earth.

Ometecuhtli is often pictured in the codices as half-man, half-woman. He appears in this Tonalamatl in his manifestation as Mictlantecuhtli, Lord of the Land of the Dead.

In her consort's absence Omecihuatl is shown here as patron of Week One Crocodile. Like Ometecuhtli she represents unity through sexual dualism. As mistress of the Thirteen Heavens, she chooses mortals' birthdays and thus their names and fates. Omecihuatl is also called Citlallicue, the Star Skirt.

In the illustration based on the Codex Nuttall, Omecihuatl holds a bag representing wealth in her left hand; the bird-footed object in her right is frequently encountered and may be an emblem of her power. Her other accoutrements—the beaked bird helmet, the bundle-like ornament on her back, the earspool, large pendant, and sandals—are standard items of Aztec divine/noble attire.

IV. TONALAMATL—A BOOK OF DAYS

WEEK TWO

ONE JAGUAR

Augury: uncertain blessings; those born in this week may tend to the immoral; unlucky week

Patron: Quetzalcoatl, the Plumed Serpent, god of learning, justice and mercy, penitence, growth and vegetation, and fertility. Barren women prayed to him. His principle temple was the enormous pyramid in Cholula (modern Puebla). While humans were sacrificed to many of the Aztec gods, and in particularly large numbers to Huitzilopochtli, Quetzalcoatl was opposed to the practice. Only birds were sacrificed in his honor.

Quetzalcoatl was a god-man, a shamanic warrior hero, miraculously conceived through his mother Chalchiuhtlicue, the Jade Skirt, finding a jade stone. The legend of Huitzilopochtli's supernatural conception may have its roots this older myth. These miraculous conceptions and that of the Spaniards' sacrificed god-man were part of a fatal mythological coincidence for the Aztecs.

In the Aztec cosmology, Quetzalcoatl lifted the heavens to reveal the earth, thus creating the Second Sun of which he was ruler. Another legend has it that on his death Quetzalcoatl became the planet Venus and eight days later rose from the dead as the morning star. Again the Spaniards' resurrected god coincided with the Aztec myth.

As Tlahuizcalpantecuhtli, Lord of the House of the Dawn, Quetzalcoatl is god of the East (the direction from which the Spaniards came), with a birth day-name of One Reed. He also manifests as Ehecatl, the God of the Wind, who represents the ephemeral, spiritual breath, power over matter, and reconciliation of opposites. Temples to Ehecatl were round as opposed to square or oblong as for other gods. Cast as Quetzalcoatl's evil twin was Xolotl, the Evening Star.

With ancient connections to the Mayan plumed serpent Kulkulkan, Quetzalcoatl was credited with bringing civilization to the peoples of Meso-America, both introducing metal working and providing the calendar. He was the main god of the Toltecs of Tula, whose priest-rulers were also named Quetzalcoatl. It was in Toltec times that the legend arose of his departure into the east and promised return in the year One Reed.

One Reed was the year in which the Aztecs welcomed the Spaniards into Tenochtitlan with exquisite gifts believing that their god had returned. It is also the year in which the Spaniards took the Aztec ruler hostage and assassinated him.

The illustration is based on both Codex Borbonicus and Codex Magliabecchi. The blond-bearded god Quetzalcoatl wears a plumed serpent on his back. The conical hat was peculiar to him and may indicate Huaxtec influences. The flowering shinbone at his forehead is a symbol of penitence. The small figure on the cape under the serpent's body is the symbol of the morning star. The cross-like figure on his shield, common in connection with Quetzalcoatl, was yet another mythical coincidence. For the fatalistic Aztecs the sudden appearance of the Spaniards in their midst had all the trappings of an epiphany.

Special days in Week One Jaguar:

One Jaguar: those born on this day (with this birth day-name) are destined for sacrifice.

Four Earthquake is the birth day-name and feast day of Tonatiuh, the Fifth Sun.

Seven Flower: day favorable to scribes and weavers.

Nine Wind is the birth day-name and feast day of Mixcoatl, the Cloud Serpent, who is both god of the Hunt and of numbers and magicians. It is an unlucky day. The festival of Mixcoatl begins the fourteenth agricultural month.

IV. TONALAMATL — A BOOK OF DAYS

17

WEEK THREE

ONE DEER

Augury: lucky week

Patron: Tepeyollotl, The Heart of the Mountain, cause of earthquakes, avalanches, and volcanos. He is the sun under the earth at night and is sometimes seen as a jaguar whose howling is the coming of sunrise. Tepeyollotl is also known as the Lord of Jewels.

This illustration combines pose and details from several codices to re-create the god.

Special days in Week One Deer:

One Deer is the birth day-name and feast day of Xochiquetzal.

Two Rabbit: day of drunkenness, fertility.

IV. TONALAMATL—A BOOK OF DAYS

19

WEEK FOUR

ONE FLOWER

Augury: cheerful, men born in this week are artistic and the women promiscuous; lucky week

Patron: Huehuecoyotl, the Old Coyote, a trickster full of craftiness; gaiety in sex, exuberance in ornamentation; he brings unexpected pleasure, sorrow, and strange happenings. He can lead one into trouble.

The Aztec Huehuecoyotl is clearly related to the mythological trickster Coyote in the legends of the desert Southwest of the United States.

The illustration incorporates pose and details from Codex Nuttall into a new image of Huehuecoyotl. The staff, seemingly inappropriate since it is a symbol of Chicomecoatl, Seven Snake, is included here as an authentic design element from the Codex.

IV. TONALAMATL — A BOOK OF DAYS

21

WEEK FIVE

ONE REED

Augury: danger of drowning, of things falling by accident; unlucky week

Patron: Chalchiuhtlicue, the Jade Skirt, goddess of the flowing waters, lakes, and whirlpools. She is unpredictable and can be a danger. As the deity of Spring, she is patron of child-rearing, youth, and beauty, as well as goddess of the East. Her festival begins the sixth agricultural month. Chalchiuhtlicue was the ruler of the Fourth Sun and mother of Quetzalcoatl.

Chalchiuhtlicue is the consort of Tlaloc. Thus there were many local Jade Skirts as the spirits of various streams and brooks and as wives of the local rain gods. In this respect, she is also the goddess of storms and forces of nature.

There were purification ceremonies in the rites for Chalchiuhtlicue which struck the Spanish clergy as very similar to the sacrament of baptism.

Chalchiuhtlicue was known in Tlaxcala as Matlalcueye, the Blue Robe. Her birth day-name is One Water.

The illustration is based on Codex Fejervary-Mayer with elements from Codex Borgia. In other images her flowing skirts sometimes contain drowning warriors.

Special days in Week One Reed:

One Reed is the birth day-name and feast day of Quetzalcoatl.

IV. TONALAMATL—A BOOK OF DAYS

WEEK SIX

ONE DEATH

Augury: neutral as to luck

Patron: Tecciztecatl, the old man moon (metztli). God of hunters, he appears as things that shine in the night. The Mexica promoted Coyolxauhqui, the sister of their god, as a moon goddess, but she did not enter into the calendar of the Turquoise Year.

This new image of the god Tecciztecatl is adapted from pose and details in Codex Nuttall. The moon-face is purely invention: rather than a face, the Aztecs saw the shape of a rabbit in the full moon. The large shell pendant is the symbol of the moon. Tecciztecatl holds a bag of sacred copal incense in his right hand. In some codices he wears butterfly wings.

Special days in Week One Death:

One Death is the birth day-name and feast day of Tezcatlipoca.

Four Water is the day-name and feast day of the Fourth Sun, ruled by Chalchiuhtlicue.

IV. TONALAMATL — A BOOK OF DAYS

25

WEEK SEVEN

ONE RAIN

Augury: warriors may be in danger; good for farmers; lucky week

Patron: Tlaloc, the Rain God, god of thunder and lightning, sender of the clouds, and god of weather in general. As provider of moisture, he is also god of fertility and vegetation. He both brings and cures rheumatic and respiratory diseases. Tlaloc is keeper of the eighth paradise in the South and was ruler of the Third Sun. He is often symbolized by the frog. Festivals for Tlaloc begin the first, third, thirteenth, and sixteenth agricultural months.

Historically, Tlaloc was the principle god of ancient Teotihuacan and is connected to the Mayan rain god Chac. In Aztec times there were many lesser local tlalocs who inhabited various hilltops and were paired with local Jade Skirts. The tlalocs controlled the area rains, lightning, thunder, snow, and hail. One such tlaloc is Quiahuitl, the nineteenth day-sign.

The illustration is based on Codex Nuttall. The long teeth, curled nose, and black face are standard in images of Tlaloc.

Special days in Week One Rain:

One Rain: very unlucky day on which the Cihuateteo, spirits of women who die in childbirth, bring illness to children.

Four Wind is the day-name and feast day of the Second Sun, ruled by Quetzalcoatl. It is a day favorable to magicians.

Seven Snake (Chicomecoatl) is the birth day-name and feast day of the guardian goddess of corn, also known as Xilonen.

IV. TONALAMATL — A BOOK OF DAYS

27

WEEK EIGHT

ONE GRASS

Augury: threatening, witchcraft, darkness, sinfulness, unhealthiness; those born in this week are in danger; very unlucky week

Patron: Mayauel, Goddess of Pulque.

Pulque or octli was a liquor made from the fermented juice of the maguey plant (metl). In the legend, Mayauel observes a mouse drinking from an injured maguey. Noting that the mouse appears to be very happy and fearless, she and her husband also drink the juice and thus discover pulque.

Among the Mexica drinking was generally permitted only in ceremonies, and otherwise drunkenness was severely punished. However, the elderly were free to drink whenever they wished. Deities of drunkenness, legion for all kinds of intoxication, were frequently referred to as the Octli gods or the "400 rabbits." Other important Octli gods were Patecatl, Totochtin, Tepoztecatl, and Macuiltochtli (Five Rabbit).

The illustration is based on Codex Nuttall and is a composite of several female figures. The rabbit has been added to represent the day of which Mayauel is patron.

IV. TONALAMATL—A BOOK OF DAYS

WEEK NINE

ONE SNAKE

Augury: life and death in balance, life cannot reach perfection, wheel of fate; an uncertain week, but lucky for merchants and travelers

Patron: Xiuhtecuhtli, the Lord of the Turquoise, the god of life-giving fire. As lord of the Turquoise Year and of time, he determines mortals' day of death and watches over departed souls on their journey to Mictlan. Xiuhtecuhtli is also lord of the blue sky of day, the unfathomable, the limitless, and unity and completion. In Aztec astronomy as lord of the Pole Star, he is the center of all things, the spindle of the universe. Xiuhtecuhtli is the consort of Chantico, the goddess of the home, and is god of the West. As Ixcoxcauhqui, He of the Yellow Face, his festivals begin the tenth and eighteenth agricultural months. His birth day-name is One Rabbit.

Xiuhtecuhtli is related to Huehueteotl, the Old God as god of fire of the hearth and home.
   The illustration is based on Codex Borbonicus. A flaming crest has been added.

Special days in Week One Snake:

One Snake: day particularly favorable for merchants and traders. A class among the Aztecs called the pochteca, they had their own special god Yacatecuhtli who was worshipped as a bundle of travelling staves and often portrayed as having a very long nose.

Nine Reed is the birth day-name and feast day of Tlazolteotl.

IV. TONALAMATL — A BOOK OF DAYS

31

WEEK TEN

ONE FLINT

Augury: unexpected destruction, bitterness of cold, harsh punishment; very unlucky week

Patron: Mictlantecuhtli, Lord of the Land of the Dead.

Souls coming to Mictlan were not warriors, who on their death joined Tonatiuh in the Fourth Heaven, nor anyone drowned or buried, who went to Tlaloc's eighth paradise. Led by the dog, souls bound for Mictlan travelled for four years crossing eight hills and nine rivers.

The illustration is based on Codex Nuttall. The bare jawbone and sacrificial knife stuck into the nose are standard in images of Mictlantecuhtli.

Special days in Week One Flint:

One Flint is the birth day-name and feast day of Huitzilopochtli.

IV. TONALAMATL—A BOOK OF DAYS

CELEBRATE NATIVE AMERICA

WEEK ELEVEN

ONE MONKEY

Augury: separation of spirit and body; lucky week, but the Cihuateteo can also return with sickness for the young

Patron: Patecatl, god of medicine and surgery, also can give comfort in illness. As the Aztecs utilized psychotropic mushrooms and herbs in their ceremonies, Patecatl is also the god of that type of intoxication and is included as a pulque/octli god among the 400 rabbits.

The illustration is based on Codex Nuttall.

Special days in Week One Monkey:

Four Jaguar is the day-name and feast day of the First Sun, ruled by Tezcatlipoca.

IV. TONALAMATL — A BOOK OF DAYS

35

WEEK TWELVE

ONE LIZARD

Augury: young men may lose their way, but find it again; can be destructive; somewhat lucky week, unpredictable

Patron: Tezcatlipoca, the Smoking Mirror, as Itzcoliuhqui, the Obsidian Blade, lord of the night sky. He is the god of the shadow side of life. He controls human life for good and ill, being loving and vengeful, but forgiving; bringing sin and anguish, but bestowing wealth and courage; inspiring order, but also fomenting quarrels; providing, but also depriving. Tezcatlipoca is the protector of slaves, god of magicians, and god of the North, and brings and cures incurable and contagious diseases. He is identified with the constellation of the Great Bear. In his disguise as a jaguar, he is patron of the Jaguar knights of the night. His festivals begin the fifth, ninth, and twelfth agricultural months. The birth day-name of Tezcatlipoca is One Death.

In legend Tezcatlipoca created the First Sun by pulling Cipactli, the Earth Monster, out of the primal waters. In this struggle he lost a foot to her but tore off her lower jaw. He was later the enemy of Quetzalcoatl and drove him from his temple in Tula, bringing down the Toltec empire. This is clearly a reference to a Toltec ruler of that name.

Tezcatlipoca was extremely important to the Aztecs with many names such as the One at the Shoulder, the Traveler, and He Who Is Everywhere. (The last was also the name that the sage-prince of Texcoco Nezahualcoyotl used to refer to his very radical concept of a single supreme being.)

Other gods were sometimes seen as his manifestations: Huitzilopochtli was called the Blue Tezcatlipoca, Xipe Totec the Red, and Quetzalcoatl the Green. In a rite for this powerful and mysterious god, priests would pray around a smooth box of sand, in which the sudden appearance of his single footprint would augur the presence of Tezcatlipoca.

Tezcatlipoca may also be Yaotl, God of Darkness, and he also appears in this Tonalamatl as Chalchiuhtotolin, the Jade Turkey.

The illustration is largely from the Codex Borgia. Tezcatlipoca's emblematic smoking mirror (made of obsidian) replaces his missing foot. The item on his left arm is the symbol of the night sky.

Special days in Week One Lizard:

Five Rabbit (Macuiltochtli) is the birth day-name and feast day of one of the innumerable gods of drunkenness.

IV. TONALAMATL — A BOOK OF DAYS

WEEK THIRTEEN

ONE EARTHQUAKE

Augury: possible danger, pleasure and death; birth of things; control of youth and warriors; neutral as to luck

Patron: Tlazolteotl, the Goddess of Filth, absolver of sins. As an earth mother, Tlazolteotl is also the goddess of child-bearing, but as Ixcuina, the Two-Faced, she is also patron of witchcraft, evil, and cruelty; goddess of luxury, of lustful sex and debauchery, but also of purification. Her festival begins the eleventh agricultural month, and her birth day-name is Nine Reed.

Tlazolteotl under the name Tlaelcuani, Eater of Dirt, can absolve all sins, great and small, though only once in one's life. Penitents, who often waited until they were quite old, offered copal incense with their confessions to the goddess. Having confessed, they would receive a "ticket" as official pardon for any prior offenses but sometimes had to perform severe acts of penance, including self-mutilation.

This Aztec rite impressed the Spanish clergy as similar to their sacrament of confession. Nor were other parallels to their holy sacraments lost on the priests. Among these were a ceremony of confirmation and an extreme kind of communion wherein sacrificial victims were often ritually cannibalized after yielding up their hearts to the god.

Tlazolteotl is also called Tonantzin, the Earth Mother, or Our Grandmother. In this persona she is goddess of medicine, herbs, and healing, and is sometimes worshipped as the Earth Monster Cipactli.

She is the mother of certain other deities. Her androgynous son Centeotl is god of the sprouting corn, of good promise, honesty, generosity, harvest and grain, sustenance, and healing plants. His festival begins the fourth agricultural month. Her daughter Chicomecoatl, Seven Snake, is guardian of the corn and is sometimes named Xilonen, Young Ears of Maize. Her festival begins the eighth agricultural month. Xochiquetzal, the Flower Feather, is also a daughter of Tlazolteotl.

The illustration, a composite based on Codex Nuttall, includes a volute on her staff as a symbol of penitence, a fan signifying luxury, and an infant with intact umbilical cord. Many early images of Tlazolteotl giving birth are far more graphic.

IV. TONALAMATL — A BOOK OF DAYS

WEEK FOURTEEN

ONE DOG

Augury: good for warriors, dangerous for priestly occupations, conquest of cities; very lucky week

Patron: Xipe Totec, the Flayed Lord. He is god of spring and renewal, the order of Nature, and of rain and moisture. He is lord of the sunset, as well as the spirit of liberation. Xipe Totec brings and cures boils and skin diseases. His festival begins the second agricultural month, and he is also called the Red Tezcatlipoca.

Xipe Totec is called the savior of mankind because he suffered terribly, including skinning himself, to save humanity. His origin is probably in an early maize god, and the flaying ritual represents the husking of the ears.

The illustration is based on Codex Borbonicus. It clearly shows Xipe Totec wearing the flayed skin of a sacrificial victim. The shield device of the eagle represents the day of which Xipe Totec is patron.

IV. TONALAMATL—A BOOK OF DAYS

41

WEEK FIFTEEN

ONE HOUSE

Augury: temples are darkened; the Cihuateteo appear again; very unlucky

Patron: Itzpapalotl, the Obsidian Butterfly, ancestral goddess of the stars. An air spirit, she is the lady of mystery and death, but also a goddess of beauty and fertility. She is goddess of the North and related to Tecciztecatl, the god of the moon.

As Itzacihuatl, the Obsidian Lady, she is goddess of volcanos and elemental violence, bringing terror, death, and the evil of the nightmare.

The illustration is based on Codex Borbonicus. The replacement of original feathered wings with those of the tropical butterfly Armandia Lidderdalei is an invention. Itzpapalotl holds a sacrificial flint knife.

IV. TONALAMATL—A BOOK OF DAYS

WEEK SIXTEEN

ONE VULTURE

Augury: creative, precious, and destructive, sex and death; a lucky but inconsistent week

Patron: Xolotl, the Evening Star, Quetzalcoatl's evil twin, god of malice, treachery, and danger. He is the opposite of intellect, representing the animal aspect of behavior and the darkness of the unconscious. God of ill-fortune, twins, and monstrosities, Xolotl also brings the eclipse and is a danger to mankind.

The Aztecs, ardent astronomers, had very closely calculated the cycle of Venus and were aware that the Morning and Evening Stars are the same planet at opposite ends of its cycle. This phenomenon in the heavens symbolized well for them the philosophical division between good and evil.

Frequently encountered with both Quetzalcoatl and Xolotl in the codices is a young warrior god named Piltzintecuhtli, lord of the planet Mercury, who is always subordinate to them and cyclically dives into the sun to be reborn. Astronomical observations of the Pleiades were also used to regulate the solar calendar.

In the illustration, a composite adapted from Codex Nuttall, Xolotl's monstrous aspect is defined by the traditional reversal of hands and feet and augmented by the addition of a hunched back. No connection between Xolotl and Kokopelli, the legendary humpbacked flute player of the desert Southwest, is intended. The symbol on his staff is that of the Evening Star.

Special days in Week One Vulture:

One Vulture: those born on this day will live long and happily.

Five Flower (Macuilxochitl) is the birth day-name and feast day of the god of games and gambling. His sacred game is patolli, which is played on a board patterned in a cross. The son of Xochiquetzal and Xochipilli, Macuilxochitl is a god of drunkenness and gluttony, festivals, music and singing, as well as of normal births. He brings and cures hemorrhoids and venereal diseases.

Four Rain is the day-name and feast day of the Third Sun, ruled by Tlaloc.

IV. TONALAMATL — A BOOK OF DAYS

45

CELEBRATE NATIVE AMERICA

WEEK SEVENTEEN

ONE WATER

Augury: unlucky week

Patron: Chalchiuhtotolin, the Jade Turkey, a manifestation of Tezcatlipoca as the patron of power and glory for young warriors. He is a trickster who plays a flute in the night. One who happens to see Chalchiuhtotolin must sieze him and demand to be granted a wish.

The illustration is a composite adapted from details in Codex Nuttall.

Special days in Week One Water:

One Water is the birth day-name and feast day of Chalchiuhtlicue.

IV. TONALAMATL — A BOOK OF DAYS

WEEK EIGHTEEN

ONE WIND

Augury: good omens; lucky week

Patron: Chantico, the Lady of the House (hearth fire). As the goddess of cooking, eating, and domesticity, she represents the feminine side of life, the waters of birth, the fire of spirit, fertility, and self-sacrifice. She is the patron of weaving, which was an art of women. As the consort of Xiuhtecuhtli, Chantico is also the lady of wealth and jewels.

The illustration is based on Codex Nuttall and includes a bird on her forehead. A specific omen bird was attributed to each Aztec deity and was often included in the headdress. Chantico holds a spindle as a symbol of weaving. Beautifully colored mantles woven of fine cotton served as an important item of Aztec tribute and trade.

Special days in Week One Wind:

One Wind: those with this birth day-name become astrologers, sorcerers, cast out spells, turn into animals.

IV. TONALAMATL — A BOOK OF DAYS

49

WEEK NINETEEN

ONE EAGLE

Augury: salvation through pain and suffering, the Cihuateteo are abroad again; those born in this week can be prideful; a generally unlucky week

Patron: Xochiquetzal, the Flower Feather. She is the goddess of love, of artistic inspiration, and the beauty of the feminine, as well as the patron of prostitutes and inspiring the violent emotions of sex. Xochiquetzal is also the goddess of pregnancy and children, of flowers, agriculture, and fertility. She brings and cures infections and is goddess of the West. Her birth day-name is One Deer.

Xochiquetzal is also worshipped as a goddess of Mictlan who has even more beautiful flowers in the underworld. Marigolds, thought to come from the Land of the Dead, were sacred to Xochiquetzal and still are used in contemporary Mexican traditions on All Souls Eve.

The illustration is based on Codex Borbonicus. The figure emerging from Xochiquetzal's mouth is the symbol of speech or song (cuciatl). In the original a large red serpent symbolizing sex protrudes from between her legs.

IV. TONALAMATL — A BOOK OF DAYS

51

WEEK TWENTY

ONE RABBIT

Augury: those born in this week will be prosperous, but perhaps with a weakness for drink; lucky week

Patron: Xochipilli, the Prince of Flowers. Consort of Xochiquetzal, Xochipilli is god of laughter and happiness, feasting and dancing, pleasure and frivolity. He is the god of beauty and peace, ecstacy, sleep, and dreams, as well as of flowers, gardens, and agriculture. Xochipilli is also god of the sacred ball game tlachtli which was played with a six-inch solid rubber ball and symbolized the vicissitudes of fate and fortune.

Although the patron of this week is generally cited as Itzli, the Knife, inasmuch as Xochipilli has a role in other accounts of the Turquoise Year, this more interesting and palatable deity is substituted as patron of Week One Rabbit. The illustration is based on Codex Nuttall. The comb-like headdress is distinctive of Xochipilli, and the song symbol cuciatl and flowers are standard.

Special days in Week One Rabbit:

One Rabbit is the birth day-name and feast day of Xiuhtecuhtli.

IV. TONALAMATL—A BOOK OF DAYS

53

IV.

THE AZTEC CENTURY COUNT

▲▼

THE SACRED CALENDAR OF THE AZTECS also counts a "century" which consists of 52 Turquoise Years (37 solar years plus six days). This larger sacred cycle was enumerated in a familiar pattern of four 13-year "decades" (palli).

Each Turquoise Year is designated by one of four day-signs which serve as year-signs: Rabbit, Reed, Flint, and House - in the constant order shown to the right.

The turn of a century was a landmark event for the Aztecs as they literally waited to see if the world would continue for another cycle. Even when the new cycle effectively seemed to have begun, nothing was considered certain until the year Two Reed was reached. Then the reprieve was celebrated with the New Fire ceremony.

The four year-signs apparently also have divinatory significance, though it is only known that Rabbit years were viewed as tending to hardship and famine. There is also a correspondence between the year-bearers and the four elements: Rabbit - Earth, Reed - Water, Flint - Air, and House - Fire. In addition each of the four cardinal directions is associated with a particular year-bearer.

THE AZTEC COUNT OF YEARS

First Palli:

1 RABBIT	2 REED	3 FLINT	4 HOUSE
5 RABBIT	6 REED	7 FLINT	8 HOUSE
9 RABBIT	10 REED	11 FLINT	12 HOUSE
13 RABBIT			

Second Palli:

	1 REED	2 FLINT	3 HOUSE
4 RABBIT	5 REED	6 FLINT	7 HOUSE
8 RABBIT	9 REED	10 FLINT	11 HOUSE
12 RABBIT	13 REED		

Third Palli:

		1 FLINT	2 HOUSE
3 RABBIT	4 REED	5 FLINT	6 HOUSE
7 RABBIT	8 REED	9 FLINT	10 HOUSE
11 RABBIT	12 REED	13 FLINT	

Fourth Palli:

			1 HOUSE
2 RABBIT	3 REED	4 FLINT	5 HOUSE
6 RABBIT	7 REED	8 FLINT	9 HOUSE
10 RABBIT	11 REED	12 FLINT	13 HOUSE

SOUTH: location of Tlaloc's eighth heaven
Augury: fertility and growing, but also can be evil
Patron: Ometecuhtli and Omecihuatl (The Mexica also promoted Huitzilopochtli as the patron of the South.)
Related year: Rabbit

EAST: home of dead warriors and the Morning Star
Augury: abundance, rebirth
Patron: Quetzalcoatl and Chalchiuhtlicue
Related year: Reed

NORTH: direction of ill omen
Augury: mystery, possibly evil, darkness
Patron: Tezcatlipoca and Itzpapalotl
Related year: Flint

WEST: home of the Cihuateteo and the Earth Monster Cipactli
Augury: lucky, but also linked to death and Xolotl
Patron: Xiuhtecuhtli and Xochiquetzal
Related year: House

V.
THE SIXTH SUN

AFTER LANDING ON THE GULF COAST OF Mexico in April, 1519, Hernán Cortés led his small band of conquistadors inland to Tenochtitlan. In that historic encounter Cortés siezed the Revered Speaker Moctezuma Xocoyotzin, the Younger, and murdered him. Expelled from the city, the Spaniards fought on for two years to capture Tenochtitlan and, in the end of ends, only succeeded with the aid of the subject peoples. When the city fell, the last Revered Speaker, Cuauhtemoc, the Eagle Descending, was also murdered. However, almost 20 years of war were waged before the Spaniards subjugated the entire Aztec domain.

Tenochtitlan fell on August 13, 1521. This is a fitting date to mark the end of the Aztec Fifth Sun. August 13, 1521 was day One Snake of Turquoise Year Three House. Continuing the count, August 14 would have been Two Death; August 15 Three Deer, etc. It is easy to imagine that somewhere descendants of the Aztecs continued the sacred Tonalpohualli of the Fifth Sun in this way, though their world seemed to have come to an end.

It is often said that in every end there is a beginning. In this sense the day after the fall of Tenochtitlan, August 14, 1521, was the birth of a new Sun, the Sixth Sun. A new Sun for Native America, it has begun with many trials and sufferings for the indigenous populations of the western hemisphere. A new epoch, the Sixth Sun can still bring forth a new and wonderful expression of the cultures of Native America as its cycles continue their progression. The Tonalpohualli of the Turquoise Year, when counted in the present time, can reframe time and human fortune through its sacred cycles.

Many centuries of the Sixth Sun have already passed. It is time to give this Sun a name. Honoring the traditional mythology of Four Jaguar, Four Rain, etc., let the birth day-name of the Sixth Sun be Nahuixochitl, Four Flower. The Sixth Sun thus can be described by the auguries of the day Flower: it is the symbol of the soul, holy and evanescent.

The patron deities of Nahuixochitl, the Sixth Sun, are the divine pair Xochiquetzal, Flower Feather, and Xochipilli, Prince of Flowers. Together they foster love and happiness, artistic inspiration, fertility, pleasure, feasting, music, dancing, beauty, and peace. Their metaphor is human life as a flower: growing, blooming, fading. Four Flower, the feast day of the Sixth Sun, is to be celebrated in the joyous spirit of its divine rulers.

To further establish the Tonalpohualli of the Sixth Sun, the centuries that have elapsed must be counted. Although it is not known how the Aztecs actually counted their centuries, the earlier Mayan calendar indicates that they most likely were grouped in larger cycles or eras. A tradition exists that the Fifth Sun was composed of four separate periods, each under the rule of a deity. The first was the era of Xochiquetzal, and the second was that of Quetzalcoatl. The Aztecs lived in the third era, that of Tezcatlipoca, and anticipated the fourth to begin upon the return of Quetzalcoatl.

If certain day-signs are also used as century-bearers to run a ritual count of "Turquoise Centuries" paralleling the pattern of day-signs as year-bearers, logical candidates for these hypothetical century-bearers would be Dog, Eagle, Flower, and Snake, in this order.

A 52-count of Turquoise Centuries from One Dog through Thirteen Snake establishes an era of 1,925 solar years less 66 days. The traditional four palli of the century count reoccur in the count of the era. Thus the first era of the Sixth Sun contains four ages of 481 solar years plus 75 days. Given these calculations, it is possible to build a realistic concordance with the modern Gregorian calendar, while making allowance, however, for some curious facts:

1) In order to convert from the Julian to the Gregorian calendar in 1582, ten days were dropped, causing the day October 4 to be followed immediately by October 15. The Julian calendar was established by Julius Caesar and the Gregorian by Pope Gregory XIII.

2) Centessimal years (those ending in 00) are leap years only if divisible by 400, e. g., 1600 and 2000.

THE FIRST ERA OF FOUR FLOWER, THE SIXTH SUN

TURQUOISE CENTURY	GREGORIAN DATES
First Age:	
1 Dog	08/14/1521 - 08/19/1558
2 Eagle	08/20/1558 - 09/04/1595
3 Flower	09/05/1595 - 09/10/1632
4 Snake	09/11/1632 - 09/16/1669
5 Dog	09/17/1669 - 09/23/1706
6 Eagle	09/24/1706 - 09/29/1743
7 Flower	09/30/1743 - 10/05/1780
8 Snake	10/06/1780 - 10/12/1817
9 Dog	10/13/1817 - 10/18/1854
10 Eagle	10/19/1854 - 10/24/1891
11 Flower	10/25/1891 - 10/31/1928
12 Snake	11/01/1928 - 11/06/1965
13 Dog	11/07/1965 - 11/12/2002
Second Age:	
1 Eagle	11/13/2002 -
to 13 Eagle	- 02/10/2484
Third Age:	
1 Flower	02/11/2484 -
to 13 Flower	- 05/11/2965
Fourth Age:	
1 Snake	05/12/2965 -
to 13 Snake	- 08/10/3446

The century cycles of this first era of the Sixth Sun may prove insightful in terms of Native American history. In an overview of the First Age of Dog, the auguries of that day apply: it leads the soul through the underworld. The First Age has indeed been a journey through the underworld for Native Americans, having experienced the destructive aftermath of invasion: subjugation, generations of oppression, and the continuing struggle to survive as distinct and vital cultures.

We, in 1993, live in the last half of the century Thirteen Dog, the final years of the age of Dog, a time when the Native American peoples can at last emerge from their Mictlan into a Second Age beginning in 2002. The auguries for this age of Eagle are bravery and renewal. In 2484, the Third Age, Flower, begins hopefully, accompanied by the many desirable implications of Xochiquetzal and Xochipilli, its patron deities. In 2965, the final age of the first era of the Sixth Sun, the age of Snake, begins and promises mystical power. A more positive forecast for Native America could hardly be imagined.

A closer look into the Turquoise Centuries of the First Age and their auguries reveals correlations to events in the history of Native Americans. For example, the century Nine Dog—very unlucky/underworld—was the period of many forced migrations of tribes, a notable example of which is the Cherokee and their Trail of Tears. In the following century, Ten Eagle—bravery/renewal—Native American resistance during the Indian Wars exemplified courage and new-found strength. Other correspondences may be discovered when Native American history is viewed through these unique cycles.

A further examination of the table of Turquoise Centuries indicates that the last "decade" of century Thirteen Dog, the palli of lucky House, begins August 12, 1993. This will be a very special New Year's Day inaugurating the final cycle of the age of Dog. During this cycle of 13 Turquoise Years, the qualities of House, nobility and intelligence, will be required of all peoples in this vast land to prepare for the auspicious new age of Eagle.

In honor of the heritage of and hopes for Native America, the Concordance Tables of the Turquoise Centuries Twelve Snake and Thirteen Dog which follow provide the means for discovering our Sixth Sun birth day-names and new birthdays in the tradition and spirit of these early Native Americans, the Aztecs.

There are, of course, also occasions to commemorate the mythical epochs of humankind in America. According to the concordance tables, the festival day-names and dates of the several Suns in the first year One House will be:

Four Earthquake, the Fifth Sun	August 28, 1993
Four Water, the Fourth Sun	October 19, 1993
Four Wind, the Second Sun	November 1, 1993
Four Jaguar, the First Sun	December 23, 1993
Four Flower, the Sixth Sun	January 18, 1994
Four Rain, the Third Sun	February 26, 1994.

Since the new year Two Rabbit begins on April 29, 1994, the day-names of the Suns in that year shift noticeably:

Four Earthquake, the Fifth Sun	May 15, 1994
Four Water, the Fourth Sun	July 6, 1994
Four Wind, the Second Sun	July 19, 1994
Four Jaguar, the First Sun	September 9, 1994
Four Flower, the Sixth Sun	October 5, 1994
Four Rain, the Third Sun	November 13, 1994.

By restoring these ceremonial occasions in the tonalpohualli of the Sixth Sun to the present, there is now great opportunity to celebrate the multifaceted heritage of Native America.

EPILOGUE

THE CULTURAL IDENTITY CRISIS NOW confronting the United States is a direct result of the country trying to be a "melting pot" of its various immigrant cultures. Unfortunately, all that process succeeds in producing is a homogenized mass of marketing myths and consumerism.

In spite of decades of attempting to "melt" everyone into a single American culture, the contemporary United States still remains aggressively multicultural. Far more appropriate is the metaphor of the country as a "stew pot" which preserves and enhances the flavors of its diverse ingredients with all their unique cultures and heritages. These differences are the fertile ground in which our cultural identities grow. Celebrating the many unique peoples in this country well serves its prophetic motto, "E Pluribus Unum," in many one.

And first of all it is indeed proper to celebrate the cultures of Native America, the peoples inhabiting these continents before the European encounter. Willy nilly, Native Americans became host to the hordes of newcomers to their shores. Now after centuries of displacement and containment, they remain host, like it or not, to the hundreds of millions of today's New Americans.

As in any large-scale mixing of peoples, the past five centuries of contacts between the idigenes and the immigrants have supplied Native American ancestors for a geometric progression of descendants. Far more of today's New Americans share a strain of Native American blood than would ever suspect. A great many family trees include some ancestor at least in part of Indian stock, someone often purposely obscured in the New American family lore.

Yet all New Americans, regardless of any possible blood tie, have very good reason to respect and celebrate the Native American heritage. It is a priceless legacy for us all, a wealth of wisdom about the nature of reality, spirituality, and faithful stewardship of this earth on which we but dwell.

CELEBRATE NATIVE AMERICA

TO IDENTIFY A DATE in the Turquoise calendar, find the week within which it falls. For example, December 1, 1928 falls in week One Deer. Then turn to the illustration of that week in the Tonalamatl (in this instance, page 19) and run the count: One Deer, 11/27; Two Rabbit, 11/28; Three Water, 11/29; Four Dog, 11/30; and Five Monkey, 12/01.

TABLE I

CONCORDANCE OF CENTURY 12 SNAKE AND FIRST THREE PALLI OF CENTURY 13 DOG (by WEEK)

CENTURY 12 DOG

First Palli:

1 RABBIT
1 Cro 11/01/28
1 Jag 11/14
1 Deer 11/27
1 Flo 12/10
1 Reed 12/23/28
1 Dea 01/05/29
1 Rain 01/18
1 Gra 01/31
1 Sna 02/13
1 Fli 02/26
1 Mon 03/11
1 Liz 03/24
1 Ear 04/06
1 Dog 04/19
1 Hou 05/02
1 Vul 05/15
1 Wat 05/28
1 Wind 06/10
1 Eag 06/23
1 Rab 07/06/29

2 REED
1 Cro 07/19/29
1 Jag 08/01
1 Deer 08/14
1 Flo 08/27
1 Reed 09/09
1 Dea 09/22
1 Rain 10/05
1 Gra 10/18
1 Sna 10/31
1 Fli 11/13
1 Mon 11/26
1 Liz 12/09
1 Ear 12/22/29
1 Dog 01/04/30
1 Hou 01/17
1 Vul 01/30
1 Wat 02/12
1 Wind 02/25
1 Eag 03/10
1 Rab 03/23/30

3 FLINT
1 Cro 04/05/30
1 Jag 04/18
1 Deer 05/01
1 Flo 05/14
1 Reed 05/27
1 Dea 06/09
1 Rain 06/22
1 Gra 07/05
1 Sna 07/18
1 Fli 07/31
1 Mon 08/13
1 Liz 08/26
1 Ear 09/08
1 Dog 09/21
1 Hou 10/04
1 Vul 10/17
1 Wat 10/30
1 Wind 11/12
1 Eag 11/25
1 Rab 12/08/30

4 HOUSE
1 Cro 12/21/30
1 Jag 01/03/31
1 Deer 01/16
1 Flo 01/29
1 Reed 02/11
1 Dea 02/24
1 Rain 03/09
1 Gra 03/22
1 Sna 04/04
1 Fli 04/17
1 Mon 04/30
1 Liz 05/13
1 Ear 05/26
1 Dog 06/08
1 Hou 06/21
1 Vul 07/04
1 Wat 07/17
1 Wind 07/30
1 Eag 08/12
1 Rab 08/25/31

5 RABBIT
1 Cro 09/07/31
1 Jag 09/20
1 Deer 10/03
1 Flo 10/16
1 Reed 10/29
1 Dea 11/11
1 Rain 11/24
1 Gra 12/07
1 Sna 12/20/31
1 Fli 01/02/32
1 Mon 01/15
1 Liz 01/28
1 Ear 02/10
1 Dog 02/23
1 Hou 03/07
1 Vul 03/20
1 Wat 04/02
1 Wind 04/15
1 Eag 04/28
1 Rab 05/11/32

6 REED
1 Cro 05/24/32
1 Jag 06/06
1 Deer 06/19
1 Flo 07/02
1 Reed 07/15
1 Dea 07/28
1 Rain 08/10
1 Gra 08/23
1 Sna 09/05
1 Fli 09/18
1 Mon 10/01
1 Liz 10/16
1 Ear 10/27
1 Dog 11/09
1 Hou 11/22
1 Vul 12/07
1 Wat 12/18
1 Wind 12/31/32
1 Eag 01/13/33
1 Rab 01/26/33

7 FLINT
1 Cro 02/08/33
1 Jag 02/21
1 Deer 03/06
1 Flo 03/19
1 Reed 04/01
1 Dea 04/14
1 Rain 04/27
1 Gra 05/10
1 Sna 05/23
1 Fli 06/05
1 Mon 06/18
1 Liz 07/01
1 Ear 07/14
1 Dog 07/27
1 Hou 08/09
1 Vul 08/22
1 Wat 09/04
1 Wind 09/17
1 Eag 09/30
1 Rab 10/13/33

8 HOUSE
1 Cro 10/26/33
1 Jag 11/08
1 Deer 11/21
1 Flo 12/04
1 Reed 12/17
1 Dea 12/30/33
1 Rain 01/12/34
1 Gra 01/25
1 Sna 02/07
1 Fli 02/20
1 Mon 03/05
1 Liz 03/18
1 Ear 03/31
1 Dog 04/13
1 Hou 04/26
1 Vul 05/09
1 Wat 05/22
1 Wind 06/04
1 Eag 06/17
1 Rab 06/30/34

9 RABBIT
1 Cro 07/13/34
1 Jag 07/26
1 Deer 08/08
1 Flo 08/21
1 Reed 09/03
1 Dea 09/16
1 Rain 09/29
1 Gra 10/12
1 Sna 10/25
1 Fli 11/07
1 Mon 11/20
1 Liz 12/03
1 Ear 12/16
1 Dog 12/29/34
1 Hou 01/11/35
1 Vul 01/24
1 Wat 02/06
1 Wind 02/19
1 Eag 03/04
1 Rab 03/17/35

10 REED
1 Cro 03/30/35
1 Jag 04/12
1 Deer 04/25
1 Flo 05/08
1 Reed 05/21
1 Dea 06/03
1 Rain 06/16
1 Gra 06/29
1 Sna 07/12
1 Fli 07/25
1 Mon 08/07
1 Liz 08/20
1 Ear 09/02
1 Dog 09/15
1 Hou 09/28
1 Vul 10/11
1 Wat 10/24
1 Wind 11/06
1 Eag 11/19
1 Rab 12/02/35

11 FLINT
1 Cro 12/15/35
1 Jag 12/28/35
1 Deer 01/10/36
1 Flo 01/23
1 Reed 02/05
1 Dea 02/18
1 Rain 03/02
1 Gra 03/15
1 Sna 03/28
1 Fli 04/10
1 Mon 04/23
1 Liz 05/06
1 Ear 05/19
1 Dog 06/01
1 Hou 06/14
1 Vul 06/27
1 Wat 07/10
1 Wind 07/23
1 Eag 08/05
1 Rab 08/18/36

12 HOUSE
1 Cro 08/31/36
1 Jag 09/13
1 Deer 09/26
1 Flo 10/09
1 Reed 10/22
1 Dea 11/04
1 Rain 11/17
1 Gra 11/30
1 Sna 12/13
1 Fli 12/26/36
1 Mon 01/08/37
1 Liz 01/21
1 Ear 02/03
1 Dog 02/16
1 Hou 03/01
1 Vul 03/14
1 Wat 03/27
1 Wind 04/09
1 Eag 04/22
1 Rab 05/05/37

13 RABBIT
1 Cro 05/18/37
1 Jag 05/31
1 Deer 06/13
1 Flo 06/26
1 Reed 07/09
1 Dea 07/22
1 Rain 08/04
1 Gra 08/17
1 Sna 08/30
1 Fli 09/12
1 Mon 09/25
1 Liz 10/08
1 Ear 10/21
1 Dog 11/03
1 Hou 11/16
1 Vul 11/29
1 Wat 12/12
1 Wind 12/25/37
1 Eag 01/07/38
1 Rab 01/20/38

Second Palli:

1 REED
1 Cro 02/02/38
1 Jag 02/15
1 Deer 02/28
1 Flo 03/12
1 Reed 03/26
1 Dea 04/08
1 Rain 04/21
1 Gra 05/04
1 Sna 05/17
1 Fli 05/30
1 Mon 06/12
1 Liz 06/25
1 Ear 07/08
1 Dog 07/21
1 Hou 08/03
1 Vul 08/16
1 Wat 08/29
1 Wind 09/11
1 Eag 09/24
1 Rab 10/07/38

2 FLINT
1 Cro 10/20/38
1 Jag 11/02
1 Deer 11/15
1 Flo 11/28
1 Reed 12/11
1 Dea 12/24/38
1 Rain 01/06/39
1 Gra 01/19
1 Sna 02/01
1 Fli 02/14
1 Mon 02/27
1 Liz 03/12
1 Ear 03/25
1 Dog 04/07
1 Hou 04/20
1 Vul 05/03
1 Wat 05/16
1 Wind 05/29
1 Eag 06/11
1 Rab 06/24/39

3 HOUSE
1 Cro 07/07/39
1 Jag 07/20
1 Deer 08/02
1 Flo 08/15
1 Reed 08/28
1 Dea 09/10
1 Rain 09/23
1 Gra 10/06
1 Sna 10/19
1 Fli 11/01
1 Mon 11/14
1 Liz 11/27
1 Ear 12/10
1 Dog 12/23/39
1 Hou 01/05/40
1 Vul 01/18
1 Wat 01/31
1 Wind 02/13
1 Eag 02/26
1 Rab 03/10/40

4 RABBIT
1 Cro 03/23/40
1 Jag 04/05
1 Deer 04/18
1 Flo 05/01
1 Reed 05/14
1 Dea 05/27
1 Rain 06/09
1 Gra 06/22
1 Sna 07/05
1 Fli 07/18
1 Mon 07/31
1 Liz 08/13
1 Ear 08/26
1 Dog 09/08
1 Hou 09/21
1 Vul 10/04
1 Wat 10/17
1 Wind 10/30
1 Eag 11/12
1 Rab 11/25/40

5 REED
1 Cro 12/08/40
1 Jag 12/21/40
1 Deer 01/03/41
1 Flo 01/16
1 Reed 01/29
1 Dea 02/11
1 Rain 02/24
1 Gra 03/09
1 Sna 03/22
1 Fli 04/04
1 Mon 04/17
1 Liz 04/30
1 Ear 05/13
1 Dog 05/26
1 Hou 06/08
1 Vul 06/21
1 Wat 07/04
1 Wind 07/17
1 Eag 07/30
1 Rab 08/12/41

6 FLINT
1 Cro 08/25/41
1 Jag 09/07
1 Deer 09/20
1 Flo 10/03
1 Reed 10/16
1 Dea 10/29
1 Rain 11/11
1 Gra 11/24
1 Sna 12/07
1 Fli 12/20/41
1 Mon 01/02/42
1 Liz 01/15
1 Ear 01/28
1 Dog 02/10
1 Hou 02/23
1 Vul 03/08
1 Wat 03/21
1 Wind 04/03
1 Eag 04/16
1 Rab 04/29/42

7 HOUSE
1 Cro 05/12/42
1 Jag 05/25
1 Deer 06/07
1 Flo 06/20
1 Reed 07/03
1 Dea 07/16
1 Rain 07/29
1 Gra 08/11
1 Sna 08/24
1 Fli 09/06
1 Mon 09/19
1 Liz 10/02
1 Ear 10/15
1 Dog 10/28
1 Hou 11/10
1 Vul 11/23
1 Wat 12/06
1 Wind 12/19/42
1 Eag 01/01/43
1 Rab 01/14/43

8 RABBIT
1 Cro 01/27/43
1 Jag 02/09
1 Deer 02/22
1 Flo 03/07
1 Reed 03/20
1 Dea 04/02
1 Rain 04/15
1 Gra 04/28
1 Sna 05/11
1 Fli 05/24
1 Mon 06/06
1 Liz 06/18
1 Ear 07/02
1 Dog 07/15
1 Hou 07/28
1 Vul 08/10
1 Wat 08/23
1 Wind 09/05
1 Eag 09/18
1 Rab 10/01/43

9 REED
1 Cro 10/14/43
1 Jag 10/27
1 Deer 11/09
1 Flo 11/22
1 Reed 12/05
1 Dea 12/18
1 Rain 12/31/43
1 Gra 01/13/44
1 Sna 01/26
1 Fli 02/08
1 Mon 02/21
1 Liz 03/05
1 Ear 03/18
1 Dog 03/31
1 Hou 04/13
1 Vul 04/26
1 Wat 05/09
1 Wind 05/22
1 Eag 06/04
1 Rab 06/17/44

10 FLINT
1 Cro 06/30/44
1 Jag 07/13
1 Deer 07/26
1 Flo 08/08
1 Reed 08/21
1 Dea 09/03
1 Rain 09/16
1 Gra 09/29
1 Sna 10/12
1 Fli 10/25
1 Mon 11/07
1 Liz 11/20
1 Ear 12/03
1 Dog 12/16
1 Hou 12/29/44
1 Vul 01/11/45
1 Wat 01/24
1 Wind 02/06
1 Eag 02/19
1 Rab 03/04/45

11 HOUSE
1 Cro 03/17/45
1 Jag 03/30
1 Deer 04/12
1 Flo 04/25
1 Reed 05/08
1 Dea 05/21
1 Rain 06/03
1 Gra 06/16
1 Sna 06/29
1 Fli 07/12
1 Mon 07/25
1 Liz 08/07
1 Ear 08/20
1 Dog 09/02
1 Hou 09/15
1 Vul 09/28
1 Wat 10/11
1 Wind 10/24
1 Eag 11/06
1 Rab 11/19/45

12 RABBIT
1 Cro 12/02/45
1 Jag 12/15
1 Deer 12/28/45
1 Flo 01/10/46
1 Reed 01/23
1 Dea 02/05
1 Rain 02/18
1 Gra 03/03
1 Sna 03/16
1 Fli 03/29
1 Mon 04/11
1 Liz 04/24
1 Ear 05/07
1 Dog 05/20
1 Hou 06/02
1 Vul 06/15
1 Wat 06/28
1 Wind 07/11
1 Eag 07/24
1 Rab 08/06/46

13 REED
1 Cro 08/19/46
1 Jag 09/01
1 Deer 09/14
1 Flo 09/27
1 Reed 10/10
1 Dea 10/23
1 Rain 11/05
1 Gra 11/18
1 Sna 12/01
1 Fli 12/14
1 Mon 12/27/46
1 Liz 01/09/47
1 Ear 01/22
1 Dog 02/04
1 Hou 02/17
1 Vul 03/02
1 Wat 03/15
1 Wind 03/28
1 Eag 04/10
1 Rab 04/23/47

Third Palli:

1 FLINT
1 Cro 05/06/47
1 Jag 05/19
1 Deer 06/01
1 Flo 06/14
1 Reed 06/27
1 Dea 07/10
1 Rain 07/23
1 Gra 08/05
1 Sna 08/18
1 Fli 08/31
1 Mon 09/13
1 Liz 09/26
1 Ear 10/09
1 Dog 10/22
1 Hou 11/04
1 Vul 11/17
1 Wat 11/30
1 Wind 12/13
1 Eag 12/26/47
1 Rab 01/08/48

2 HOUSE
1 Cro 01/21/48
1 Jag 02/03
1 Deer 02/16
1 Flo 02/29
1 Reed 03/13
1 Dea 03/26
1 Rain 04/08
1 Gra 04/21
1 Sna 05/04
1 Fli 05/17
1 Mon 05/30
1 Liz 06/12

CELEBRATE NATIVE AMERICA

1 Ear 06/25	1 Dea 05/15	8 REED	1 Hou 04/01	1 Gra 02/19	3 REED	1 Hou 12/11	1 Gra 10/30	1 Jag 10/01	1 Wat 09/16	1 Jag 04/24	1 Wat 04/08
1 Dog 07/08	1 Rain 05/28	1 Cro 04/29/52	1 Vul 04/14	1 Sna 03/03	1 Cro 01/08/58	1 Vul 12/24/59	1 Sna 11/12	1 Deer 10/15	1 Wind 09/29	1 Deer 05/07	1 Wind 04/21
1 Hou 07/21	1 Gra 06/10	1 Jag 05/12	1 Wat 04/27	1 Fli 03/16	1 Jag 01/21	1 Wat 01/06/60	1 Fli 11/25	1 Flo 10/28	1 Eag 10/12	1 Flo 05/20	1 Eag 05/04
1 Vul 08/03	1 Sna 06/23	1 Deer 05/25	1 Wind 05/10	1 Mon 03/29	1 Deer 02/03	1 Wind 01/19	1 Mon 12/08	1 Reed 11/10	1 Rab 10/25/65	1 Reed 06/02	1 Rab 05/17/69
1 Wat 08/16	1 Fli 07/06	1 Flo 06/07	1 Eag 05/23	1 Liz 04/11	1 Flo 02/16	1 Eag 02/01	1 Liz 12/21/61	1 Dea 11/23		1 Dea 06/15	
1 Wind 08/29	1 Mon 07/19	1 Reed 06/20	1 Rab 06/05/54	1 Ear 04/24	1 Reed 03/01	1 Ear 01/03/62	1 Rain 12/06		1 Rain 06/28	6 REED
1 Eag 09/11	1 Liz 08/01	1 Dea 07/03		1 Dog 05/07	1 Dea 03/14	1 Dog 01/16	1 Gra 12/19/63		1 Gra 07/11	1 Cro 05/30/69
1 Rab 09/24/48	1 Ear 08/14	1 Rain 07/16	11 RABBIT	1 Hou 05/20	1 Rain 03/27	1 Hou 01/29	1 Sna 01/01/64		1 Sna 07/24	1 Jag 06/12
	1 Dog 08/27	1 Gra 07/29	1 Cro 06/18/54	1 Vul 06/02	6 RABBIT	1 Vul 02/11	1 Fli 01/14	CENTURY	1 Fli 08/06	1 Deer 06/25
3 RABBIT	1 Hou 09/09	1 Jag 07/01	1 Deer 07/14	1 Wat 06/15	1 Cro 02/27/60	1 Wat 02/24	1 Mon 01/27	13 DOG	1 Mon 08/19	1 Flo 07/08
1 Cro 10/07/48	1 Vul 09/22	1 Sna 08/11	1 Fli 08/24	1 Wind 06/28	1 Jag 03/11	1 Wind 03/09	1 Liz 02/09		1 Liz 09/01	1 Reed 07/21
1 Jag 10/20	1 Wat 10/05	1 Fli 08/24	1 Mon 09/06	1 Eag 07/11	1 Deer 03/24	1 Eag 03/22	1 Ear 02/22	First Palli:	1 Ear 09/14	1 Dea 08/03
1 Deer 11/02	1 Wind 10/18	1 Mon 09/06	1 Liz 09/19	1 Rab 07/24/56	1 Flo 04/06	1 Rab 04/04/62	1 Dog 03/06	1 RABBIT	1 Dog 09/27	1 Rain 08/16
1 Flo 11/15	1 Eag 10/31	1 Liz 09/19	1 Ear 10/02		1 Reed 04/19		1 Hou 03/19	1 Cro 11/07/65	1 Hou 10/10	1 Gra 08/29
1 Reed 11/28	1 Rab 11/13/50	1 Ear 10/02	1 Dog 10/15	Fourth Palli:	1 Dea 05/02	9 HOUSE	1 Vul 04/01	1 Jag 11/20	1 Vul 10/23	1 Sna 09/11
1 Dea 12/11		1 Dog 10/15	1 Hou 10/28	1 HOUSE	1 Rain 05/15	1 Cro 04/17/62	1 Wat 04/14	1 Deer 12/03	1 Wat 11/05	1 Fli 09/24
1 Rain 12/24/48	6 HOUSE	1 Hou 10/28	1 Vul 11/10	1 Cro 08/06/56	1 Gra 05/28	1 Jag 04/30	1 Wind 04/27	1 Flo 12/16	1 Wind 11/18	1 Mon 10/07
1 Gra 01/06/49	1 Cro 11/26/50	1 Vul 11/10	1 Wat 11/23	1 Jag 08/19	1 Sna 06/10	1 Deer 05/13	1 Eag 05/10	1 Reed 12/29/65	1 Eag 12/01	1 Liz 10/20
1 Sna 01/19	1 Jag 12/09	1 Wat 11/23	1 Wind 12/06	1 Deer 09/01	1 Fli 06/23	1 Flo 05/26	1 Rab 05/23/64	1 Dea 01/11/66	1 Rab 12/14/67	1 Ear 11/02
1 Fli 02/01	1 Deer 12/22/50	1 Wind 12/06	1 Eag 12/19/52	1 Flo 09/14	1 Mon 07/06	1 Reed 06/08		1 Rain 01/24		1 Dog 11/15
1 Mon 02/14	1 Flo 01/04/51	1 Eag 12/19/52	1 Rab 01/01/53	1 Reed 09/27	1 Liz 07/19	1 Dea 06/21	12 FLINT	1 Gra 02/06	4 HOUSE	1 Hou 11/28
1 Liz 02/27	1 Reed 01/17	1 Rab 01/01/53		1 Dea 10/10	1 Ear 08/01	1 Rain 07/04	1 Cro 06/05/64	1 Sna 02/19	1 Cro 12/27/67	1 Vul 12/11
1 Ear 03/12	1 Dea 01/30		9 FLINT	1 Rain 10/23	1 Dog 08/14	1 Gra 07/17	1 Jag 06/18	1 Fli 03/04	1 Jag 01/09/68	1 Wat 12/23/69
1 Dog 03/25	1 Rain 02/12		1 Cro 01/14/53	1 Gra 11/05	1 Hou 08/27	1 Sna 07/30	1 Deer 07/01	1 Mon 03/17	1 Deer 01/22	1 Wind 01/06/70
1 Hou 04/07	1 Gra 02/25		1 Jag 01/27	1 Sna 11/18	1 Vul 09/09	1 Fli 08/12	1 Flo 07/14	1 Liz 03/30	1 Flo 02/04	1 Eag 01/19
1 Vul 04/20	1 Sna 03/10		1 Deer 02/09	1 Fli 12/01	1 Wat 09/22	1 Mon 08/25	1 Reed 07/27	1 Ear 04/12	1 Reed 02/17	1 Rab 02/01/70
1 Fli 05/03	1 Fli 03/23		1 Flo 02/22	1 Mon 12/14	1 Wind 10/05	1 Liz 09/07	1 Dea 08/09	1 Dog 04/25	1 Dea 03/01	
1 Wat 05/03	1 Mon 04/05		1 Reed 03/07	1 Liz 12/27/56	1 Eag 10/18	1 Ear 09/20	1 Rain 08/22	1 Hou 05/08	1 Rain 03/14	7 FLINT
1 Wind 05/16	1 Liz 04/18		1 Dea 03/20	1 Ear 01/09/57	1 Rab 10/31/60	1 Dog 10/03	1 Gra 09/04	1 Vul 05/21	1 Gra 03/27	1 Cro 02/14/70
1 Eag 05/29	1 Ear 05/01		1 Rain 04/02	1 Dog 01/22		1 Hou 10/16	1 Sna 09/17	1 Wat 06/03	1 Sna 04/09	1 Jag 02/27
1 Rab 06/11/49	1 Dog 05/14		1 Gra 04/15	1 Hou 02/04	7 REED	1 Vul 10/29	1 Fli 09/30	1 Wind 06/16	1 Fli 04/22	1 Deer 03/12
	1 Hou 05/27	12 REED	1 Sna 04/28	1 Vul 02/17	1 Cro 11/13/60	1 Wat 11/11	1 Mon 10/13	1 Eag 06/29	1 Mon 05/05	1 Flo 03/25
4 REED	1 Vul 06/09	1 Cro 03/05/55	1 Fli 05/11	1 Wat 03/02	1 Jag 11/26	1 Wind 11/24	1 Liz 10/26	1 Rab 07/12/66	1 Liz 05/18	1 Reed 04/07
1 Cro 06/24/49	1 Wat 06/22	1 Jag 03/18	1 Mon 05/24	1 Wind 03/15	1 Deer 12/09	1 Eag 12/07	1 Ear 11/08		1 Ear 05/31	1 Dea 04/20
1 Jag 07/07	1 Wind 07/05	1 Deer 03/31	1 Liz 06/06	1 Eag 03/28	1 Flo 12/22/60	1 Rab 12/20/62	1 Dog 11/21	2 REED	1 Dog 06/13	1 Rain 05/03
1 Deer 07/20	1 Eag 07/18	1 Flo 04/13	1 Reed 06/19	1 Rab 04/10/57	1 Reed 01/04/61		1 Hou 12/04	1 Cro 07/25/66	1 Hou 06/26	1 Gra 05/16
1 Flo 08/02	1 Rab 07/31/51	1 Reed 04/26	1 Ear 07/02		1 Dea 01/17	10 RABBIT	1 Vul 12/17	1 Jag 08/07	1 Vul 07/09	1 Sna 05/29
1 Reed 08/15		1 Dea 05/09	1 Dog 07/02	2 RABBIT	1 Rain 01/30	1 Cro 01/02/63	1 Wat 12/30/64	1 Deer 08/20	1 Wat 07/22	1 Fli 06/11
1 Dea 08/28	7 RABBIT	1 Rain 05/22	1 Hou 07/15	1 Cro 04/23/57	1 Gra 02/12	1 Jag 01/15	1 Wind 01/12/65	1 Flo 09/02	1 Wind 08/04	1 Mon 06/24
1 Rain 09/10	1 Cro 08/13/51	1 Gra 06/04	1 Vul 07/28	1 Jag 05/06	1 Sna 02/25	1 Deer 01/28	1 Eag 01/25	1 Reed 09/15	1 Eag 08/17	1 Liz 07/07
1 Gra 09/23	1 Jag 08/26	1 Sna 06/17	1 Wat 08/10	1 Deer 05/19	1 Fli 03/10	1 Flo 02/10	1 Rab 02/07/65	1 Dea 09/28	1 Rab 08/30/68	1 Ear 07/20
1 Sna 10/06	1 Deer 09/08	1 Fli 06/30	1 Wind 08/23	1 Flo 06/01	1 Mon 03/23	1 Reed 02/23				1 Dog 08/02
1 Fli 10/19	1 Flo 09/21	1 Mon 07/13	1 Eag 09/05	1 Reed 06/14	1 Liz 04/05	1 Dea 03/08	13 HOUSE	5 RABBIT		1 Hou 08/15
1 Mon 11/01	1 Reed 10/04	1 Liz 07/26	1 Rab 09/18/53	1 Dea 06/27	1 Ear 04/18	1 Rain 03/21	1 Cro 02/20/65	1 Rain 10/11		1 Vul 08/28
1 Liz 11/14	1 Dea 10/17	1 Ear 08/08		1 Rain 07/10	1 Dog 05/01	1 Gra 04/03	1 Jag 03/05	1 Cro 09/12/68		1 Wat 09/10
1 Ear 11/27	1 Rain 10/30	1 Dog 08/21	10 HOUSE	1 Gra 07/23	1 Hou 05/14	1 Sna 04/16	1 Deer 03/18	1 Jag 09/25		1 Wind 09/23
1 Dog 12/10	1 Gra 11/12	1 Hou 09/03	1 Cro 10/01/53	1 Sna 08/05	1 Vul 05/27	1 Fli 04/29	1 Flo 03/31	1 Deer 10/08		1 Eag 10/06
1 Hou 12/23/49	1 Sna 11/25	1 Vul 09/16	1 Jag 10/14	1 Fli 08/18	1 Wat 06/09	1 Mon 05/12	1 Liz 04/13	1 Flo 10/21		1 Rab 10/19/70
1 Vul 01/05/50	1 Fli 12/08	1 Wat 09/29	1 Deer 10/27	1 Mon 08/31	1 Wind 06/22	1 Liz 05/25	1 Ear 04/26	1 Reed 11/03		
1 Wat 01/18	1 Mon 12/21/51	1 Wind 10/12	1 Flo 11/09	1 Liz 09/13	1 Eag 07/05	1 Ear 06/07	1 Dog 05/09	1 Dea 11/16		8 HOUSE
1 Wind 01/31	1 Liz 01/03/52	1 Eag 10/25	1 Reed 11/22	1 Ear 07/29	1 Rab 07/18/61	1 Dog 06/20	1 Hou 05/22	1 Rain 11/29		1 Cro 11/01/70
1 Eag 02/13	1 Ear 01/16	1 Rab 11/07/55	1 Dea 12/05	1 Dog 10/09		1 Hou 07/03	1 Vul 02/05	1 Gra 12/12		1 Jag 11/14
1 Rab 02/26/50	1 Dog 01/29		1 Rain 12/18	1 Hou 10/22	8 FLINT	1 Vul 07/16	1 Wat 02/18	1 Sna 12/25/68		1 Deer 11/27
	1 Hou 02/11	13 FLINT	1 Gra 12/31/53	1 Vul 11/04	1 Cro 07/31/61	1 Wat 07/29	1 Wind 03/03	1 Fli 01/07/69		1 Flo 12/10
5 FLINT	1 Vul 02/24	1 Cro 11/20/55	1 Sna 01/13/54	1 Fli 10/07	1 Jag 08/13	1 Wind 08/11	1 Mon 06/30	1 Mon 01/20		1 Reed 12/23/70
1 Cro 03/11/50	1 Wat 03/08	1 Jag 12/03	1 Fli 01/26	1 Mon 10/20	1 Deer 08/26	1 Eag 08/24	1 Liz 07/13	1 Eag 03/16		1 Dea 01/05/71
1 Jag 03/24	1 Wind 03/21	1 Deer 12/16	1 Mon 02/08	1 Liz 11/02	1 Flo 09/08	1 Rab 09/06/63	1 Ear 07/26	1 Rab 03/29/69		1 Rain 01/18
1 Deer 04/06	1 Eag 04/03	1 Flo 12/29/55	1 Liz 02/21	1 Wat 11/17	1 Reed 09/21		1 Dog 08/08			1 Gra 01/31
1 Flo 04/19	1 Rab 04/16/52	1 Reed 01/11/56	1 Ear 03/06	1 Wind 11/30	1 Dea 10/04	11 REED	1 Hou 08/21	3 FLINT		1 Sna 02/13
1 Reed 05/02		1 Dea 01/24	1 Dog 03/19	1 Eag 12/13	1 Rain 10/17	1 Cro 09/19/63	1 Vul 09/03	1 Cro 04/11/67	1 Vul 03/26	
		1 Rain 02/06		1 Rab 12/26/57						

60

CONCORDANCE TABLES

1 Fli 02/26
1 Mon 03/11
1 Liz 03/24
1 Ear 04/06
1 Dog 04/19
1 Hou 05/02
1 Vul 05/15
1 Wat 05/28
1 Wind 06/10
1 Eag 06/23
1 Rab 07/06/71

9 RABBIT
1 Cro 07/19/71
1 Jag 08/01
1 Deer 08/14
1 Flo 08/27
1 Reed 09/09
1 Dea 09/22
1 Rain 10/05
1 Gra 10/18
1 Sna 10/31
1 Fli 11/13
1 Mon 11/26
1 Liz 12/09
1 Ear 12/22/71
1 Dog 01/04/72
1 Hou 01/17
1 Vul 01/30
1 Wat 02/12
1 Wind 02/25
1 Eag 03/09
1 Rab 03/22/72

10 REED
1 Cro 04/04/72
1 Jag 04/17
1 Deer 04/30
1 Flo 05/13
1 Reed 05/26
1 Dea 06/08
1 Rain 06/21
1 Gra 07/04
1 Sna 07/17
1 Fli 07/30
1 Mon 08/12
1 Liz 08/25
1 Ear 09/07
1 Dog 09/20
1 Hou 10/03
1 Vul 10/16
1 Wat 10/29
1 Wind 11/11
1 Eag 11/24
1 Rab 12/07/72

11 FLINT
1 Cro 12/20/72
1 Jag 01/02/73
1 Deer 01/15

1 Flo 01/28
1 Reed 02/10
1 Dea 02/23
1 Rain 03/08
1 Gra 03/21
1 Sna 04/03
1 Fli 04/16
1 Mon 04/29
1 Liz 05/12
1 Ear 05/25
1 Dog 06/07
1 Hou 06/20
1 Vul 07/03
1 Wat 07/16
1 Wind 07/29
1 Eag 08/11
1 Rab 08/24/73

12 HOUSE
1 Cro 09/06/73
1 Jag 09/19
1 Deer 10/02
1 Flo 10/15
1 Reed 10/28
1 Dea 11/10
1 Rain 11/23
1 Gra 12/06
1 Sna 12/19/73
1 Fli 01/01/74
1 Mon 01/14
1 Liz 01/27
1 Ear 02/09
1 Dog 02/22
1 Hou 03/07
1 Vul 03/20
1 Wat 04/02
1 Wind 04/15
1 Eag 04/28
1 Rab 05/11/74

13 RABBIT
1 Cro 05/24/74
1 Jag 06/06
1 Deer 06/19
1 Flo 07/02
1 Reed 07/15
1 Dea 07/28
1 Rain 08/10
1 Gra 08/23
1 Sna 09/05
1 Fli 09/18
1 Mon 10/01
1 Liz 10/14
1 Ear 10/27
1 Dog 11/09
1 Hou 11/22
1 Vul 12/05
1 Wat 12/18
1 Wind 12/31/74

1 Eag 01/13/75
1 Rab 01/26/75

Second Palli:
1 REED
1 Cro 02/08/75
1 Jag 02/21
1 Deer 03/06
1 Flo 03/19
1 Reed 04/01
1 Dea 04/14
1 Rain 04/27
1 Gra 05/10
1 Sna 05/23
1 Fli 06/05
1 Mon 06/18
1 Liz 07/01
1 Ear 07/14
1 Dog 07/27
1 Hou 08/09
1 Vul 08/22
1 Wat 09/04
1 Wind 09/17
1 Eag 09/30
1 Rab 10/13/75

2 FLINT
1 Cro 10/26/75
1 Jag 11/08
1 Deer 11/21
1 Flo 12/04
1 Reed 12/17
1 Dea 12/30/75
1 Rain 01/12/76
1 Gra 01/25
1 Sna 02/07
1 Fli 02/20
1 Mon 03/04
1 Liz 03/17
1 Ear 03/30
1 Dog 04/12
1 Hou 04/25
1 Vul 05/08
1 Wat 05/21
1 Wind 06/03
1 Eag 06/16
1 Rab 06/29/76

3 HOUSE
1 Cro 07/12/76
1 Jag 07/25
1 Deer 08/07
1 Flo 08/20
1 Reed 09/02
1 Dea 09/15
1 Rain 09/28

1 Mon 11/19
1 Liz 12/02
1 Ear 12/15
1 Dog 12/28/76
1 Hou 01/10/77
1 Vul 01/23
1 Wat 02/05
1 Wind 02/18
1 Eag 03/03
1 Rab 03/16/77

4 RABBIT
1 Cro 03/29/77
1 Jag 04/11
1 Deer 04/24
1 Flo 05/07
1 Reed 05/20
1 Dea 06/02
1 Rain 06/15
1 Gra 06/28
1 Sna 07/11
1 Fli 07/24
1 Mon 08/06
1 Liz 08/19
1 Ear 09/01
1 Dog 09/14
1 Hou 09/27
1 Vul 10/10
1 Wat 10/23
1 Wind 11/05
1 Eag 11/18
1 Rab 12/01/77

5 REED
1 Cro 12/14/77
1 Jag 12/27/77
1 Deer 01/09/78
1 Flo 01/22
1 Reed 02/04
1 Dea 02/17
1 Rain 03/02
1 Gra 03/15
1 Sna 03/28
1 Fli 04/10
1 Mon 04/23
1 Liz 05/06
1 Ear 05/19
1 Dog 06/01
1 Hou 06/14
1 Vul 06/27
1 Wat 07/10
1 Wind 07/23
1 Eag 08/05
1 Rab 08/18/78

6 FLINT
1 Cro 08/31/78
1 Jag 09/13
1 Deer 09/26

1 Flo 10/09
1 Reed 10/22
1 Dea 11/04
1 Rain 11/17
1 Gra 11/30
1 Sna 12/13
1 Fli 12/26/78
1 Mon 01/08/79
1 Liz 01/21
1 Ear 02/03
1 Dog 02/16
1 Hou 03/01
1 Vul 03/14
1 Wat 03/27
1 Wind 04/09
1 Eag 04/22
1 Rab 05/05/79

7 HOUSE
1 Cro 05/18/79
1 Jag 05/31
1 Deer 06/13
1 Flo 06/26
1 Reed 07/09
1 Dea 07/22
1 Rain 08/04
1 Gra 08/17
1 Sna 08/30
1 Fli 09/12
1 Mon 09/25
1 Liz 10/08
1 Ear 10/21
1 Dog 11/03
1 Hou 11/16
1 Vul 11/29
1 Wat 12/12
1 Wind 12/25/79
1 Eag 01/07/80
1 Rab 01/20/80

8 RABBIT
1 Cro 02/02/80
1 Jag 02/15
1 Deer 02/28
1 Flo 03/12
1 Reed 03/25
1 Dea 04/07
1 Rain 04/20
1 Gra 05/03
1 Sna 05/16
1 Fli 05/29
1 Mon 06/11
1 Liz 06/24
1 Ear 07/07
1 Dog 07/20
1 Hou 08/02
1 Vul 08/15
1 Wat 08/28
1 Fli 07/18
1 Wind 09/10

1 Eag 09/23
1 Rab 10/06/80

9 REED
1 Cro 10/19/80
1 Jag 11/01
1 Deer 11/14
1 Flo 11/27
1 Reed 12/10
1 Dea 12/23/80
1 Rain 01/05/81
1 Gra 01/18
1 Sna 01/31
1 Fli 02/13
1 Mon 02/26
1 Liz 03/11
1 Ear 03/24
1 Dog 04/06
1 Hou 04/19
1 Vul 05/02
1 Wat 05/15
1 Wind 05/28
1 Eag 06/10
1 Rab 06/23/81

10 FLINT
1 Cro 07/06/81
1 Jag 07/19
1 Deer 08/01
1 Flo 08/14
1 Reed 08/27
1 Dea 09/09
1 Rain 09/22
1 Gra 10/05
1 Sna 10/18
1 Fli 10/31
1 Mon 11/13
1 Liz 11/26
1 Ear 12/09
1 Dog 12/22/81
1 Hou 01/04/82
1 Vul 01/17
1 Wat 01/30
1 Wind 02/12
1 Eag 02/25
1 Rab 03/10/82

11 HOUSE
1 Cro 03/23/82
1 Jag 04/05
1 Deer 04/18
1 Flo 05/01
1 Reed 05/14
1 Dea 05/27
1 Rain 06/09
1 Gra 06/22
1 Sna 07/05
1 Mon 07/31

1 Eag 09/23
1 Ear 08/26
1 Dog 09/08
1 Hou 09/21
1 Cro 10/19/80
1 Jag 11/01
1 Deer 11/14
1 Flo 11/27
1 Reed 12/10
1 Dea 12/23/80
1 Rain 01/05/81
1 Gra 01/18
1 Sna 01/31
1 Fli 02/13
1 Mon 02/26
1 Liz 03/11
1 Ear 03/24
1 Dog 04/06
1 Hou 04/19
1 Vul 05/02
1 Wat 05/15
1 Wind 05/28
1 Eag 06/10
1 Rab 11/25/82

12 RABBIT
1 Cro 12/08/82
1 Jag 12/21/82
1 Deer 01/03/83
1 Flo 01/16
1 Reed 01/29
1 Dea 02/11
1 Rain 02/24
1 Gra 03/09
1 Sna 03/22
1 Fli 04/04
1 Mon 04/17
1 Liz 04/30
1 Ear 05/13
1 Dog 05/26
1 Hou 06/08
1 Vul 06/21
1 Wat 07/04
1 Wind 07/17
1 Eag 07/30
1 Rab 08/12/83

13 REED
1 Cro 08/25/83
1 Jag 09/07
1 Deer 09/20
1 Flo 10/03
1 Reed 10/16
1 Dea 10/29
1 Rain 11/11
1 Gra 11/24
1 Sna 12/07
1 Fli 12/20/83
1 Mon 01/02/84
1 Liz 01/15
1 Ear 01/28
1 Dog 02/10
1 Hou 02/23
1 Vul 03/07
1 Wat 03/20
1 Wind 04/02
1 Eag 04/15
1 Rab 04/28/84

Third Palli:
1 FLINT
1 Cro 05/11/84

1 Liz 08/13
1 Ear 08/26
1 Dog 09/08
1 Hou 09/21
1 Vul 10/04
1 Wat 10/17
1 Wind 10/30
1 Eag 11/12
1 Rab 11/25/82

12 RABBIT
1 Cro 12/08/82
1 Jag 12/21/82
1 Deer 01/03/83
1 Flo 01/16
1 Reed 01/29
1 Dea 02/11
1 Rain 02/24
1 Gra 03/09
1 Sna 03/22
1 Fli 04/04
1 Mon 04/17
1 Liz 04/30
1 Ear 05/13
1 Dog 05/26
1 Hou 06/08
1 Vul 06/21
1 Wat 07/04
1 Wind 07/17
1 Eag 07/30
1 Rab 08/12/83

13 REED
1 Cro 08/25/83
1 Jag 09/07
1 Deer 09/20
1 Flo 10/03
1 Reed 10/16
1 Dea 10/29
1 Rain 11/11
1 Gra 11/24
1 Sna 12/07
1 Fli 12/20/83
1 Mon 01/02/84
1 Liz 01/15
1 Ear 01/28
1 Dog 02/10
1 Hou 02/23
1 Vul 03/07
1 Wat 03/20
1 Wind 04/02
1 Eag 04/15
1 Rab 04/28/84

2 HOUSE
1 Cro 01/26/85
1 Jag 02/08
1 Deer 02/21
1 Flo 03/06
1 Reed 03/19
1 Dea 04/01
1 Rain 04/14
1 Gra 04/27
1 Sna 05/10
1 Fli 05/23
1 Mon 06/05
1 Liz 06/18
1 Ear 07/01
1 Dog 07/14
1 Hou 07/27
1 Vul 08/09
1 Wat 08/22
1 Wind 09/04
1 Eag 09/17
1 Rab 09/30/85

3 RABBIT
1 Cro 10/13/85
1 Jag 10/26
1 Deer 11/08
1 Flo 11/21
1 Reed 12/04
1 Dea 12/17
1 Rain 12/30/85
1 Gra 01/12/86
1 Sna 01/25
1 Fli 02/07
1 Mon 02/20
1 Liz 03/05
1 Ear 03/18
1 Dog 03/31
1 Rain 02/18
1 Gra 03/02
1 Sna 03/15

1 Jag 05/24
1 Deer 06/06
1 Flo 06/19
1 Reed 07/02
1 Dea 07/15
1 Rain 07/28
1 Gra 08/10
1 Sna 08/23
1 Fli 09/05
1 Mon 09/18
1 Liz 10/01
1 Ear 10/14
1 Dog 10/27
1 Hou 11/09
1 Vul 11/22
1 Wat 12/05
1 Wind 12/18
1 Eag 12/31/84
1 Rab 01/13/85

4 REED
1 Cro 06/30/86
1 Jag 07/13
1 Deer 07/26
1 Flo 08/08
1 Reed 08/21
1 Dea 09/03
1 Rain 09/16
1 Gra 09/29
1 Sna 10/12
1 Fli 10/25
1 Mon 11/07
1 Liz 11/20
1 Ear 12/03
1 Dog 12/16
1 Hou 12/29/86
1 Vul 01/11/87
1 Wat 01/24
1 Wind 02/06
1 Eag 02/19
1 Rab 03/04/87

5 FLINT
1 Cro 03/17/87
1 Jag 03/30
1 Deer 04/12
1 Flo 04/25
1 Reed 05/08
1 Dea 05/21
1 Rain 06/03
1 Gra 06/16
1 Sna 06/29
1 Fli 07/12
1 Mon 07/25
1 Liz 08/07
1 Ear 08/20
1 Dog 09/02
1 Hou 09/15
1 Vul 09/28
1 Wat 10/11
1 Wind 10/24
1 Eag 11/06
1 Rab 11/19/87

6 HOUSE
1 Cro 12/02/87
1 Jag 12/15
1 Deer 12/28/87
1 Flo 01/10/88
1 Reed 01/23
1 Dea 02/05

1 Wat 05/09
1 Wind 05/22
1 Eag 06/04
1 Rab 06/17/86

1 Fli 03/28
1 Mon 04/10
1 Liz 04/23
1 Ear 05/06
1 Dog 05/19
1 Hou 06/01
1 Vul 06/14
1 Wat 06/27
1 Wind 07/10
1 Eag 07/23
1 Rab 08/05/88

7 RABBIT
1 Cro 08/18/88
1 Jag 08/31
1 Deer 09/13
1 Flo 09/26
1 Reed 10/09
1 Dea 10/22
1 Rain 11/04
1 Gra 11/17
1 Sna 11/30
1 Fli 12/13
1 Mon 12/26/88
1 Liz 01/08/89
1 Ear 01/21
1 Dog 02/03
1 Hou 02/16
1 Vul 03/01
1 Wat 03/14
1 Wind 03/27
1 Eag 04/09
1 Rab 04/22/89

8 REED
1 Cro 05/05/89
1 Jag 05/18
1 Deer 05/31
1 Flo 06/13
1 Reed 06/26
1 Dea 07/09
1 Rain 07/22
1 Gra 08/04
1 Sna 08/17
1 Fli 08/30
1 Mon 09/12
1 Liz 09/25
1 Ear 10/08
1 Dog 10/21
1 Hou 11/03
1 Vul 11/16
1 Wat 11/29
1 Wind 12/12
1 Eag 12/25/89
1 Rab 01/07/90

9 FLINT
1 Cro 01/20/90
1 Jag 02/02

1 Deer 02/15
1 Flo 02/28
1 Reed 03/13
1 Dea 03/26
1 Rain 04/08
1 Gra 04/21
1 Sna 05/04
1 Fli 05/17
1 Mon 05/30
1 Liz 06/12
1 Ear 06/25
1 Dog 07/08
1 Hou 07/21
1 Vul 08/03
1 Wat 08/16
1 Wind 08/29
1 Eag 09/11
1 Rab 09/24/90

10 HOUSE
1 Cro 10/07/90
1 Jag 10/20
1 Deer 11/02
1 Flo 11/15
1 Reed 11/28
1 Dea 12/11
1 Rain 12/24/90
1 Gra 01/06/91
1 Sna 01/19
1 Fli 02/01
1 Mon 02/14
1 Liz 02/27
1 Ear 03/12
1 Dog 03/25
1 Hou 04/07
1 Vul 04/20
1 Wat 05/03
1 Wind 05/16
1 Eag 05/29
1 Rab 06/11/91

11 RABBIT
1 Cro 06/24/91
1 Jag 07/07
1 Deer 07/20
1 Flo 08/02
1 Reed 08/15
1 Dea 08/28
1 Rain 09/10
1 Gra 09/23
1 Sna 10/06
1 Fli 10/19
1 Mon 11/01
1 Liz 11/14
1 Ear 11/27
1 Dog 12/10
1 Hou 12/23/91
1 Vul 01/05/92
1 Wat 01/18

1 Wind 01/31
1 Eag 02/13
1 Rab 02/26/92

12 REED
1 Cro 03/10/92
1 Jag 03/23
1 Deer 04/05
1 Flo 04/18
1 Reed 05/01
1 Dea 05/14
1 Rain 05/27
1 Gra 06/09
1 Sna 06/22
1 Fli 07/05
1 Mon 07/18
1 Liz 07/31
1 Ear 08/13
1 Dog 08/26
1 Hou 09/08
1 Vul 09/21
1 Wat 10/04
1 Wind 10/17
1 Eag 10/30
1 Rab 11/12/92

13 FLINT
1 Cro 11/25/92
1 Jag 12/08
1 Deer 12/21/92
1 Flo 01/03/93
1 Reed 01/16
1 Dea 01/29
1 Rain 02/11
1 Gra 02/24
1 Sna 03/09
1 Fli 03/22
1 Mon 04/04
1 Liz 04/17
1 Ear 04/30
1 Dog 05/13
1 Hou 05/26
1 Vul 06/08
1 Wat 06/21
1 Wind 07/04
1 Eag 07/17
1 Rab 07/30/93

CELEBRATE NATIVE AMERICA

TABLE II

CONCORDANCE OF FOURTH PALLI OF CENTURY 13 DOG (by DAY)

#	Sign	Date	#	Sign	Date	#	Sign	Date	#	Sign	Date	#	Sign	Date	#	Sign	Date	#	Sign	Date	#	Sign	Date	#	Sign	Date	#	Sign	Date	#	Sign	Date	#	Sign	Date	#	Sign	Date
1	HOUSE		13	Gra	10/02	13	Liz	11/23	7	Hou	01/21	1	Wind	03/21	6	Rain	05/17	13	Fli	07/15	7	Ear	09/12	1	Vul	11/10	8	Eag	01/08	13	Gra	03/06	7	Mon	05/04
1	Cro	08/12/93	1	Reed	10/03	1	Sna	11/24	8	Liz	01/22	2	Hou	03/22	7	Flo	05/18	1	Rain	07/16	8	Fli	09/13	2	Ear	11/11	9	Vul	01/09	1	Reed	03/07	8	Gra	05/05
2	Wind	08/13	2	Jag	10/04	2	Dea	11/25	9	Sna	01/23	3	Liz	03/23	8	Cro	05/19	2	Flo	07/17	9	Rain	09/14	3	Fli	11/12	10	Ear	01/10	2	Jag	03/08	9	Reed	05/06
3	Hou	08/14	3	Eag	10/05	3	Deer	11/26	10	Dea	01/24	4	Sna	03/24	9	Wind	05/20	3	Cro	07/18	10	Flo	09/15	4	Rain	11/13	11	Fli	01/11	3	Eag	03/09	10	Jag	05/07
4	Liz	08/15	4	Vul	10/06	4	Rab	11/27	11	Deer	01/25	5	Dea	03/25	10	Hou	05/21	4	Wind	07/19	11	Cro	09/16	5	Flo	11/14	12	Rain	01/12	4	Vul	03/10	11	Eag	05/08
5	Sna	08/16	5	Ear	10/07	5	Wat	11/28	12	Rab	01/26	6	Deer	03/26	11	Liz	05/22	5	Hou	07/20	12	Wind	09/17	6	Cro	11/15	13	Flo	01/13/95	5	Ear	03/11	12	Vul	05/09
6	Dea	08/17	6	Fli	10/08	6	Dog	11/29	13	Wat	01/27	7	Rab	03/27	12	Sna	05/23	6	Liz	07/21	13	Hou	09/18	7	Wind	11/16				6	Fli	03/12	13	Ear	05/10
7	Deer	08/18	7	Rain	10/09	7	Mon	11/30	1	Dog	01/28	8	Wat	03/28	13	Dea	05/24	7	Sna	07/22	1	Liz	09/19	8	Hou	11/17	3	REED		7	Rain	03/13	1	Fli	05/11
8	Rab	08/19	8	Flo	10/10	8	Gra	12/01	2	Mon	01/29	9	Dog	03/29	1	Deer	05/25	8	Dea	07/23	2	Sna	09/20	9	Liz	11/18	1	Cro	01/14/95	8	Flo	03/14	2	Rain	05/12
9	Wat	08/20	9	Cro	10/11	9	Reed	12/02	3	Gra	01/30	10	Mon	03/30	2	Rab	05/26	9	Deer	07/24	3	Dea	09/21	10	Sna	11/19	2	Wind	01/15	9	Cro	03/15	3	Flo	05/13
10	Dog	08/21	10	Wind	10/12	10	Jag	12/03	4	Reed	01/31	11	Gra	03/31	3	Wat	05/27	10	Rab	07/25	4	Deer	09/22	11	Dea	11/20	3	Hou	01/16	10	Wind	03/16	4	Cro	05/14
11	Mon	08/22	11	Hou	10/13	11	Eag	12/04	5	Jag	02/01	12	Reed	04/01	4	Dog	05/28	11	Wat	07/26	5	Rab	09/23	12	Deer	11/21	4	Liz	01/17	11	Hou	03/17	5	Wind	05/15
12	Gra	08/23	12	Liz	10/14	12	Vul	12/05	6	Eag	02/02	13	Jag	04/02	5	Mon	05/29	12	Dog	07/27	6	Wat	09/24	13	Rab	11/22	5	Sna	01/18	12	Liz	03/18	6	Hou	05/16
13	Reed	08/24	13	Sna	10/15	13	Ear	12/06	7	Vul	02/03	1	Gra	04/03	6	Gra	05/30	13	Mon	07/28	7	Dog	09/25	1	Wat	11/23	6	Dea	01/19	13	Sna	03/19	7	Liz	05/17
1	Jag	08/25	1	Dea	10/16	1	Fli	12/07	8	Ear	02/04	2	Vul	04/04	7	Reed	05/31	1	Gra	07/29	8	Mon	09/26	2	Dog	11/24	7	Deer	01/20	1	Dea	03/20	8	Sna	05/18
2	Eag	08/26	2	Deer	10/17	2	Rain	12/08	9	Fli	02/05	3	Ear	04/05	8	Jag	06/01	2	Reed	07/30	9	Gra	09/27	3	Mon	11/25	8	Rab	01/21	2	Deer	03/21	9	Dea	05/19
3	Vul	08/27	3	Rab	10/18	3	Flo	12/09	10	Rain	02/06	4	Fli	04/06	9	Eag	06/02	3	Jag	07/31	10	Reed	09/28	4	Gra	11/26	9	Wat	01/22	3	Rab	03/22	10	Deer	05/20
4	Ear	08/28	4	Wat	10/19	4	Cro	12/10	11	Flo	02/07	5	Rain	04/07	10	Vul	06/03	4	Eag	08/01	11	Jag	09/29	5	Reed	11/27	10	Dog	01/23	4	Wat	03/23	11	Rab	05/21
5	Fli	08/29	5	Dog	10/20	5	Wind	12/11	12	Cro	02/08	6	Flo	04/08	11	Ear	06/04	5	Vul	08/02	12	Eag	09/30	6	Jag	11/28	11	Mon	01/24	5	Dog	03/24	12	Wat	05/22
6	Rain	08/30	6	Mon	10/21	6	Hou	12/12	13	Wind	02/09	7	Cro	04/09	12	Fli	06/05	6	Ear	08/03	13	Vul	10/01	7	Eag	11/29	12	Gra	01/25	6	Mon	03/25	13	Dog	05/23
7	Flo	08/31	7	Gra	10/22	7	Liz	12/13	1	Hou	02/10	8	Wind	04/10	13	Rain	06/06	7	Fli	08/04	1	Ear	10/02	8	Vul	11/30	13	Reed	01/26	7	Gra	03/26	1	Mon	05/24
8	Cro	09/01	8	Reed	10/23	8	Sna	12/14	2	Liz	02/11	9	Hou	04/11	1	Flo	06/07	8	Rain	08/05	2	Fli	10/03	9	Ear	12/01	1	Jag	01/27	8	Reed	03/27	2	Gra	05/25
9	Wind	09/02	9	Jag	10/24	9	Dea	12/15	3	Sna	02/12	10	Liz	04/12	2	Cro	06/08	9	Flo	08/06	3	Rain	10/04	10	Fli	12/02	2	Eag	01/28	9	Rab	03/28	3	Reed	05/26
10	Hou	09/03	10	Eag	10/25	10	Deer	12/16	4	Dea	02/13	11	Sna	04/13	3	Wind	06/09	10	Cro	08/07	4	Flo	10/05	11	Rain	12/03	3	Vul	01/29	10	Eag	03/29	4	Jag	05/27
11	Liz	09/04	11	Vul	10/26	11	Rab	12/17	5	Deer	02/14	12	Dea	04/14	4	Hou	06/10	11	Wind	08/08	5	Cro	10/06	12	Flo	12/04	4	Ear	01/30	11	Vul	03/30	5	Eag	05/28
12	Sna	09/05	12	Ear	10/27	12	Wat	12/18	6	Rab	02/15	13	Deer	04/15	5	Liz	06/11	12	Hou	08/09	6	Wind	10/07	13	Cro	12/05	5	Fli	01/31	12	Ear	03/31	6	Vul	05/29
13	Dea	09/06	13	Fli	10/28	13	Dog	12/19	7	Wat	02/16	1	Rab	04/16	6	Sna	06/12	13	Dea	08/10	7	Hou	10/08	1	Wind	12/06	6	Rain	02/01	13	Fli	04/01	7	Ear	05/30
1	Deer	09/07	1	Rain	10/29	1	Mon	12/20	8	Dog	02/17	2	Wat	04/17	7	Dea	06/13	1	Sna	08/11	8	Liz	10/09	2	Hou	12/07	7	Flo	02/02	1	Rain	04/02	8	Fli	05/31
2	Rab	09/08	2	Flo	10/30	2	Gra	12/21	9	Mon	02/18	3	Dog	04/18	8	Deer	06/14	2	Dea	08/12	9	Sna	10/10	3	Liz	12/08	8	Cro	02/03	2	Flo	04/03	9	Rain	06/01
3	Wat	09/09	3	Cro	10/31	3	Reed	12/22	10	Gra	02/19	4	Mon	04/19	9	Rab	06/15	3	Deer	08/13	10	Dea	10/11	4	Sna	12/09	9	Wind	02/04	3	Cro	04/04	10	Flo	06/02
4	Dog	09/10	4	Wind	11/01	4	Jag	12/23	11	Reed	02/20	5	Gra	04/20	10	Wat	06/16	4	Rab	08/14	11	Deer	10/12	5	Dea	12/10	10	Hou	02/05	4	Wind	04/05	11	Cro	06/03
5	Mon	09/11	5	Hou	11/02	5	Eag	12/24	12	Jag	02/21	6	Reed	04/21	11	Dog	06/17	5	Wat	08/15	12	Rab	10/13	6	Deer	12/11	11	Liz	02/06	5	Hou	04/06	12	Wind	06/04
6	Gra	09/12	6	Liz	11/03	6	Vul	12/25	13	Eag	02/22	7	Jag	04/22	12	Mon	06/18	6	Dog	08/16	13	Wat	10/14	7	Rab	12/12	12	Sna	02/07	6	Liz	04/07	13	Hou	06/05
7	Reed	09/13	7	Sna	11/04	7	Ear	12/26	1	Vul	02/23	8	Eag	04/23	13	Gra	06/19	7	Mon	08/17	1	Dog	10/15	8	Wat	12/13	13	Dea	02/08	7	Sna	04/08	1	Liz	06/06
8	Jag	09/14	8	Dea	11/05	8	Fli	12/27	2	Ear	02/24	9	Vul	04/24	1	Reed	06/20	8	Gra	08/18	2	Mon	10/16	9	Dog	12/14	1	Deer	02/09	8	Dea	04/09	2	Sna	06/07
9	Eag	09/15	9	Deer	11/06	9	Rain	12/28	3	Fli	02/25	10	Ear	04/25	2	Jag	06/21	9	Reed	08/19	3	Gra	10/17	10	Mon	12/15	2	Rab	02/10	9	Deer	04/10	3	Dea	06/08
10	Vul	09/16	10	Rab	11/07	10	Flo	12/29	4	Rain	02/26	11	Fli	04/26	3	Eag	06/22	10	Jag	08/20	4	Reed	10/18	11	Gra	12/16	3	Wat	02/11	10	Rab	04/11	4	Deer	06/09
11	Ear	09/17	11	Wat	11/08	11	Cro	12/30	5	Flo	02/27	12	Rain	04/27	4	Vul	06/23	11	Eag	08/21	5	Jag	10/19	12	Reed	12/17	4	Dog	02/12	11	Wat	04/12	5	Rab	06/10
12	Fli	09/18	12	Dog	11/09	12	Wind	12/31/93	6	Cro	02/28	13	Flo	04/28/94	5	Ear	06/24	12	Vul	10/22	6	Eag	10/20	13	Jag	12/18	5	Mon	02/13	12	Dog	04/13	6	Wat	06/11
13	Rain	09/19	13	Mon	11/10	13	Hou	01/01/94	7	Wind	03/01				6	Fli	06/25	13	Ear	08/23	7	Vul	10/21	1	Eag	12/19	6	Gra	02/14	13	Mon	04/14	7	Dog	06/12
1	Flo	09/20	1	Gra	11/11	1	Liz	01/02	8	Hou	03/02	2	RABBIT		7	Rain	06/26	1	Fli	08/24	8	Ear	10/22	2	Vul	12/20	7	Reed	02/15	1	Gra	04/15	8	Mon	06/13
2	Cro	09/21	2	Reed	11/12	2	Sna	01/03	9	Liz	03/03	1	Cro	04/29/94	8	Flo	06/27	2	Rain	08/25	9	Fli	10/23	3	Ear	12/21	8	Jag	02/16	2	Reed	04/16	9	Gra	06/14
3	Wind	09/22	3	Jag	11/13	3	Dea	01/04	10	Sna	03/04	2	Wind	04/30	9	Cro	06/28	3	Flo	08/26	10	Rain	10/24	4	Fli	12/22	9	Eag	02/17	3	Jag	04/17	10	Reed	06/15
4	Hou	09/23	4	Eag	11/14	4	Deer	01/05	11	Dea	03/05	3	Hou	05/01	10	Wind	06/29	4	Cro	08/27	11	Flo	10/25	5	Rain	12/23	10	Vul	02/18	4	Eag	04/18	11	Jag	06/16
5	Liz	09/24	5	Vul	11/15	5	Rab	01/06	12	Deer	03/06	4	Liz	05/02	11	Hou	06/30	5	Wind	08/28	12	Cro	10/26	6	Flo	12/24	11	Ear	02/19	5	Vul	04/19	12	Eag	06/17
6	Sna	09/25	6	Ear	11/16	6	Wat	01/07	13	Rab	03/07	5	Sna	05/03	12	Liz	07/01	6	Hou	08/29	13	Wind	10/27	7	Cro	12/25	12	Fli	02/20	6	Ear	04/20	13	Vul	06/18
7	Dea	09/26	7	Fli	11/17	7	Dog	01/08	1	Wat	03/08	6	Dea	05/04	13	Sna	07/02	7	Liz	08/30	1	Hou	10/28	8	Wind	12/26	13	Rain	02/21	7	Fli	04/21	1	Ear	06/19
8	Deer	09/27	8	Rain	11/18	8	Mon	01/09	2	Dog	03/09	7	Deer	05/05	1	Dea	07/03	8	Sna	08/31	2	Liz	10/29	9	Hou	12/27	1	Flo	02/22	8	Rain	04/22	2	Fli	06/20
9	Rab	09/28	9	Flo	11/19	9	Gra	01/10	3	Mon	03/10	8	Rab	05/06	2	Deer	07/04	9	Dea	09/01	3	Sna	10/30	10	Liz	12/28	2	Cro	02/23	9	Flo	04/23	3	Rain	06/21
10	Wat	09/29	10	Cro	11/20	10	Reed	01/11	4	Gra	03/11	9	Wat	05/07	3	Rab	07/05	10	Deer	09/02	4	Dea	10/31	11	Sna	12/29	3	Wind	02/24	10	Cro	04/24	4	Flo	06/22
11	Dog	09/30	11	Wind	11/21	11	Jag	01/12	5	Reed	03/12	10	Dog	05/08	4	Wat	07/06	11	Rab	09/03	5	Deer	11/01	12	Dea	12/30	4	Hou	02/25	11	Wind	04/25	5	Cro	06/23
12	Mon	10/01	12	Hou	11/22	12	Eag	01/13	6	Jag	03/13	11	Mon	05/09	5	Dog	07/07	12	Wat	09/04	6	Rab	11/02	13	Deer	12/31/94	5	Liz	02/26	12	Hou	04/26	6	Wind	06/24
						13	Vul	01/14	7	Eag	03/14	12	Gra	05/10	6	Mon	07/08	13	Dog	09/05	7	Wat	11/03	1	Rab	01/01/95	6	Sna	02/27	13	Liz	04/27	7	Hou	06/25
						1	Ear	01/15	8	Vul	03/15	13	Reed	05/11	7	Gra	07/09	1	Mon	09/06	8	Dog	11/04	2	Wat	01/02	7	Dea	02/28	1	Sna	04/28	8	Liz	06/26
						2	Fli	01/16	9	Ear	03/16	1	Jag	05/12	8	Reed	07/10	2	Gra	09/07	9	Mon	11/05	3	Dog	01/03	8	Deer	03/01	2	Dea	04/29	9	Sna	06/27
						3	Rain	01/17	10	Fli	03/17	2	Eag	05/13	9	Jag	07/11	3	Reed	09/08	10	Gra	11/06	4	Mon	01/04	9	Rab	03/02	3	Deer	04/30	10	Dea	06/28
						4	Flo	01/18	11	Rain	03/18	3	Vul	05/14	10	Eag	07/12	4	Jag	09/09	11	Reed	11/07	5	Gra	01/05	10	Wat	03/03	4	Rab	05/01	11	Deer	06/29
						5	Cro	01/19	12	Flo	03/19	4	Ear	05/15	11	Vul	07/13	5	Eag	09/10	12	Jag	11/08	6	Reed	01/06	11	Dog	03/04	5	Wat	05/02	12	Rab	06/30
						6	Wind	01/20	13	Cro	03/20	5	Fli	05/16	12	Ear	07/14	6	Vul	09/11	13	Eag	11/09	7	Jag	01/07	12	Mon	03/05	6	Dog	05/03	13	Wat	07/01

62

CONCORDANCE TABLES

1 Dog	07/02
2 Mon	07/03
3 Gra	07/04
4 Reed	07/05
5 Jag	07/06
6 Eag	07/07
7 Vul	07/08
8 Ear	07/09
9 Fli	07/10
10 Rain	07/11
11 Flo	07/12
12 Cro	07/13
13 Wind	07/14
1 Hou	07/15
2 Liz	07/16
3 Sna	07/17
4 Dea	07/18
5 Deer	07/19
6 Rab	07/20
7 Wat	07/21
8 Dog	07/22
9 Mon	07/23
10 Gra	07/24
11 Reed	07/25
12 Jag	07/26
13 Eag	07/27
1 Vul	07/28
2 Ear	07/29
3 Fli	07/30
4 Rain	07/31
5 Flo	08/01
6 Cro	08/02
7 Wind	08/03
8 Hou	08/04
9 Liz	08/05
10 Sna	08/06
11 Dea	08/07
12 Deer	08/08
13 Rab	08/09
1 Wat	08/10
2 Dog	08/11
3 Mon	08/12
4 Gra	08/13
5 Reed	08/14
6 Jag	08/15
7 Eag	08/16
8 Vul	08/17
9 Ear	08/18
10 Fli	08/19
11 Rain	08/20
12 Flo	08/21
13 Cro	08/22
1 Wind	08/23
2 Hou	08/24
3 Liz	08/25
4 Sna	08/26
5 Dea	08/27
6 Deer	08/28
7 Rab	08/29
8 Wat	08/30
9 Dog	08/31
10 Mon	09/01
11 Gra	09/02
12 Reed	09/03
13 Jag	09/04
1 Eag	09/05
2 Vul	09/06
3 Ear	09/07
4 Fli	09/08
5 Rain	09/09
6 Flo	09/10
7 Cro	09/11
8 Wind	09/12
9 Hou	09/13
10 Liz	09/14
11 Sna	09/15
12 Dea	09/16
13 Deer	09/17
1 Rab	09/18
2 Wat	09/19
3 Dog	09/20
4 Mon	09/21
5 Gra	09/22
6 Reed	09/23
7 Jag	09/24
8 Eag	09/25
9 Vul	09/26
10 Ear	09/27
11 Fli	09/28
12 Rain	09/29
13 Flo	09/30/95

4 FLINT

1 Cro	10/01/95
2 Wind	10/02
3 Hou	10/03
4 Liz	10/04
5 Sna	10/05
6 Dea	10/06
7 Deer	10/07
8 Rab	10/08
9 Wat	10/09
10 Dog	10/10
11 Mon	10/11
12 Gra	10/12
13 Reed	10/13
1 Jag	10/14
2 Eag	10/15
3 Vul	10/16
4 Ear	10/17
5 Fli	10/18
6 Rain	10/19
7 Flo	10/20
8 Cro	10/21
9 Wind	10/22
10 Hou	10/23
11 Liz	10/24
12 Sna	10/25
13 Dea	10/26
1 Deer	10/27
2 Rab	10/28
3 Wat	10/29
4 Dog	10/30
5 Mon	10/31
6 Gra	11/01
7 Reed	11/02
8 Jag	11/03
9 Eag	11/04
10 Vul	11/05
11 Ear	11/06
12 Fli	11/07
13 Rain	11/08
1 Flo	11/09
2 Cro	11/10
3 Wind	11/11
4 Hou	11/12
5 Liz	11/13
6 Sna	11/14
7 Dea	11/15
8 Deer	11/16
9 Rab	11/17
10 Wat	11/18
11 Dog	11/19
12 Mon	11/20
13 Gra	11/21
1 Reed	11/22
2 Jag	11/23
3 Eag	11/24
4 Vul	11/25
5 Ear	11/26
6 Fli	11/27
7 Rain	11/28
8 Flo	11/29
9 Cro	11/30
10 Wind	12/01
11 Hou	12/02
12 Liz	12/03
13 Sna	12/04
1 Dea	12/05
2 Deer	12/06
3 Rab	12/07
4 Wat	12/08
5 Dog	12/09
6 Mon	12/10
7 Gra	12/11
8 Reed	12/12
9 Jag	12/13
10 Eag	12/14
11 Vul	12/15
12 Ear	12/16
13 Fli	12/17
1 Rain	12/18
2 Flo	12/19
3 Cro	12/20
4 Wind	12/21
5 Hou	12/22
6 Liz	12/23
7 Sna	12/24
8 Dea	12/25
9 Deer	12/26
10 Rab	12/27
11 Wat	12/28
12 Dog	12/29
13 Mon	12/30
1 Gra	12/31/95
2 Reed	01/01/96
3 Jag	01/02
4 Eag	01/03
5 Vul	01/04
6 Ear	01/05
7 Fli	01/06
8 Rain	01/07
9 Flo	01/08
10 Cro	01/09
11 Wind	01/10
12 Hou	01/11
13 Liz	01/12
1 Sna	01/13
2 Dea	01/14
3 Deer	01/15
4 Rab	01/16
5 Wat	01/17
6 Dog	01/18
7 Mon	01/19
8 Gra	01/20
9 Reed	01/21
10 Jag	01/22
11 Eag	01/23
12 Vul	01/24
13 Ear	01/25
1 Fli	01/26
2 Rain	01/27
3 Flo	01/28
4 Cro	01/29
5 Wind	01/30
6 Hou	01/31
7 Liz	02/01
8 Sna	02/02
9 Dea	02/03
10 Deer	02/04
11 Rab	02/05
12 Wat	02/06
13 Dog	02/07
1 Mon	02/08
2 Gra	02/09
3 Reed	02/10
4 Jag	02/11
5 Eag	02/12
6 Vul	02/13
7 Ear	02/14
8 Fli	02/15
9 Rain	02/16
10 Flo	02/17
11 Cro	02/18
12 Wind	02/19
13 Hou	02/20
1 Liz	02/21
2 Sna	02/22
3 Dea	02/23
4 Deer	02/24
5 Rab	02/25
6 Wat	02/26
7 Dog	02/27
8 Mon	02/28
9 Gra	02/29
10 Reed	03/01
11 Jag	03/02
12 Eag	03/03
13 Vul	03/04
1 Ear	03/05
2 Fli	03/06
3 Rain	03/07
4 Flo	03/08
5 Cro	03/09
6 Wind	03/10
7 Hou	03/11
8 Liz	03/12
9 Sna	03/13
10 Dea	03/14
11 Deer	03/15
12 Rab	03/16
13 Wat	03/17
1 Dog	03/18
2 Mon	03/19
3 Gra	03/20
4 Reed	03/21
5 Jag	03/22
6 Eag	03/23
7 Vul	03/24
8 Ear	03/25
9 Fli	03/26
10 Rain	03/27
11 Flo	03/28
12 Cro	03/29
13 Wind	03/30
1 Hou	03/31
2 Liz	04/01
3 Sna	04/02
4 Dea	04/03
5 Deer	04/04
6 Rab	04/05
7 Wat	04/06
8 Dog	04/07
9 Mon	04/08
10 Gra	04/09
11 Reed	04/10
12 Jag	04/11
13 Eag	04/12
1 Vul	04/13
2 Ear	04/14
3 Fli	04/15
4 Rain	04/16
5 Flo	04/17
6 Cro	04/18
7 Wind	04/19
8 Hou	04/20
9 Liz	04/21
10 Sna	04/22
11 Dea	04/23
12 Deer	04/24
13 Rab	04/25
1 Wat	04/26
2 Dog	04/27
3 Mon	04/28
4 Gra	04/29
5 Reed	04/30
6 Jag	05/01
7 Eag	05/02
8 Vul	05/03
9 Ear	05/04
10 Fli	05/05
11 Rain	05/06
12 Flo	05/07
13 Cro	05/08
1 Wind	05/09
2 Hou	05/10
3 Liz	05/11
4 Sna	05/12
5 Dea	05/13
6 Deer	05/14
7 Rab	05/15
8 Wat	05/16
9 Dog	05/17
10 Mon	05/18
11 Gra	05/19
12 Reed	05/20
13 Jag	05/21
1 Eag	05/22
2 Vul	05/23
3 Ear	05/24
4 Fli	05/25
5 Rain	05/26
6 Flo	05/27
7 Cro	05/28
8 Wind	05/29
9 Hou	05/30
10 Liz	05/31
11 Sna	06/01
12 Dea	06/02
13 Deer	06/03
1 Rab	06/04
2 Wat	06/05
3 Dog	06/06
4 Mon	06/07
5 Gra	06/08
6 Reed	06/09
7 Jag	06/10
8 Eag	06/11
9 Vul	06/12
10 Ear	06/13
11 Fli	06/14
12 Rain	06/15
13 Flo	06/16/96

5 HOUSE

1 Cro	06/17/96
2 Wind	06/18
3 Hou	06/19
4 Liz	06/20
5 Sna	06/21
6 Dea	06/22
7 Deer	06/23
8 Rab	06/24
9 Wat	06/25
10 Dog	06/26
11 Mon	06/27
12 Gra	06/28
13 Reed	06/29
1 Jag	06/30
2 Eag	07/01
3 Vul	07/02
4 Ear	07/03
5 Fli	07/04
6 Rain	07/05
7 Flo	07/06
8 Cro	07/07
9 Wind	07/08
10 Hou	07/09
11 Liz	07/10
12 Sna	07/11
13 Dea	07/12
1 Deer	07/13
2 Rab	07/14
3 Wat	07/15
4 Dog	07/16
5 Mon	07/17
6 Gra	07/18
7 Reed	07/19
8 Jag	07/20
9 Eag	07/21
10 Vul	07/22
11 Ear	07/23
12 Fli	07/24
13 Rain	07/25
1 Flo	07/26
2 Cro	07/27
3 Wind	07/28
4 Hou	07/29
5 Liz	07/30
6 Sna	07/31
7 Dea	08/01
8 Deer	08/02
9 Rab	08/03
10 Wat	08/04
11 Dog	08/05
12 Mon	08/06
13 Gra	08/07
1 Reed	08/08
2 Jag	08/09
3 Eag	08/10
4 Vul	08/11
5 Ear	08/12
6 Fli	08/13
7 Rain	08/14
8 Flo	08/15
9 Cro	08/16
10 Wind	08/17
11 Hou	08/18
12 Liz	08/19
13 Sna	08/20
1 Dea	08/21
2 Deer	08/22
3 Rab	08/23
4 Wat	08/24
5 Dog	08/25
6 Mon	08/26
7 Gra	08/27
8 Reed	08/28
9 Jag	08/29
10 Eag	08/30
11 Vul	08/31
12 Ear	09/01
13 Fli	09/02
1 Rain	09/03
2 Flo	09/04
3 Cro	09/05
4 Wind	09/06
5 Hou	09/07
6 Liz	09/08
7 Sna	09/09
8 Dea	09/10
9 Deer	09/11
10 Rab	09/12
11 Wat	09/13
12 Dog	09/14
13 Mon	09/15
1 Gra	09/16
2 Reed	09/17
3 Jag	09/18
4 Eag	09/19
5 Vul	09/20
6 Ear	09/21
7 Fli	09/22
8 Rain	09/23
9 Flo	09/24
10 Cro	09/25
11 Wind	09/26
12 Hou	09/27
13 Liz	09/28
1 Sna	09/29
2 Dea	09/30
3 Deer	10/01
4 Rab	10/02
5 Wat	10/03
6 Dog	10/04
7 Mon	10/05
8 Gra	10/06
9 Reed	0/07
10 Jag	10/08
11 Eag	10/09
12 Vul	10/10
13 Ear	10/11
1 Fli	10/12
2 Rain	10/13
3 Flo	10/14
4 Cro	10/15
5 Wind	10/16
6 Hou	10/17
7 Liz	10/18
8 Sna	10/19
9 Dea	10/20
10 Deer	10/21
11 Rab	10/22
12 Wat	10/23
13 Dog	10/24
1 Mon	10/25
2 Gra	10/26
3 Reed	10/27
4 Jag	10/28
5 Eag	10/29
6 Vul	10/30
7 Ear	10/31
8 Fli	11/01
9 Rain	11/02
10 Flo	11/03
11 Cro	11/04
12 Wind	11/05
13 Hou	11/06
1 Liz	11/07
2 Sna	11/08
3 Dea	11/09
4 Dee	r11/10
5 Rab	11/11
6 Wat	11/12
7 Dog	11/13
8 Mon	11/14
9 Gra	11/15
10 Reed	11/16
11 Jag	11/17
12 Eag	11/18
13 Vul	11/19
1 Ear	11/20
2 Fli	11/21
3 Rain	11/22
4 Flo	11/23
5 Cro	11/24
6 Wind	11/25
7 Hou	11/26
8 Liz	11/27
9 Sna	11/28
10 Dea	11/29
11 Deer	11/30
12 Rab	12/01
13 Wat	12/02
1 Dog	12/03
2 Mon	12/04
3 Gra	12/05
4 Reed	12/06
5 Jag	12/07
6 Eag	12/08
7 Vul	12/09
8 Ear	12/10
9 Fli	12/11
10 Rain	12/12
11 Flo	12/13
12 Cro	12/14
13 Wind	12/15
1 Hou	12/16
2 Liz	12/17
3 Sna	12/18
4 Dea	12/19
5 Deer	12/20
6 Rab	12/21
7 Wat	12/22
8 Dog	12/23
9 Mon	12/24
10 Gra	12/25
11 Reed	12/26
12 Jag	12/27
13 Eag	12/28
1 Vul	12/29
2 Ear	12/30
3 Fli	12/31/96
4 Rain	01/01/97
5 Flo	01/02
6 Cro	01/03
7 Wind	01/04
8 Hou	01/05
9 Liz	01/06
10 Sna	01/07
11 Dea	01/08
12 Deer	01/09
13 Rab	01/10
1 Wat	01/11
2 Dog	01/12
3 Mon	01/13
4 Gra	01/14
5 Reed	01/15
6 Jag	01/16
7 Eag	01/17
8 Vul	01/18
9 Ear	01/19
10 Fli	01/20
11 Rain	01/21
12 Flo	01/22
13 Cro	01/23
1 Wind	01/24
2 Hou	01/25
3 Liz	01/26
4 Sna	01/27
5 Dea	01/28
6 Deer	01/29
7 Rab	01/30
8 Wat	01/31
9 Dog	02/01
10 Mon	02/02
11 Gra	02/03
12 Reed	02/04
13 Jag	02/05
1 Eag	02/06
2 Vul	02/07
3 Ear	02/08
4 Fli	02/09
5 Rain	02/10
6 Flo	02/11
7 Cro	02/12
8 Wind	02/13
9 Hou	02/14
10 Liz	02/15
11 Sna	02/16
12 Dea	02/17
13 Deer	02/18
1 Rab	02/19
2 Wat	02/20
3 Dog	02/21
4 Mon	02/22
5 Gra	02/23
6 Reed	02/24
7 Jag	02/25
8 Eag	02/26
9 Vul	02/27
10 Ear	02/28
11 Fli	03/01
12 Rain	03/02
13 Flo	03/03/97

6 RABBIT

1 Cro	03/04/97
2 Wind	03/05
3 Hou	03/06
4 Liz	03/07
5 Sna	03/08
6 Dea	03/09
7 Deer	03/10
8 Rab	03/11
9 Wat	03/12
10 Dog	03/13
11 Mon	03/14
12 Gra	03/15
13 Reed	03/16
1 Jag	03/17
2 Eag	03/18
3 Vul	03/19
4 Ear	03/20
5 Fli	03/21
6 Rain	03/22
7 Flo	03/23
8 Cro	03/24
9 Wind	03/25
10 Hou	03/26
11 Liz	03/27
12 Sna	03/28
13 Dea	03/29
1 Deer	03/30
2 Rab	03/31
3 Wat	04/01
4 Dog	04/02
5 Mon	04/03
6 Gra	04/04
7 Reed	04/05
8 Jag	04/06
9 Eag	04/07
10 Vul	04/08
11 Ear	04/09
12 Fli	04/10
13 Rain	04/11
1 Flo	04/12
2 Cro	04/13
3 Wind	04/14
4 Hou	04/15
5 Liz	04/16
6 Sna	04/17
7 Dea	04/18
8 Deer	04/19
9 Rab	04/20
10 Wat	04/21
11 Dog	04/22
12 Mon	04/23
13 Gra	04/24
1 Reed	04/25
2 Jag	04/26
3 Eag	04/27
4 Vul	04/28
5 Ear	04/29
6 Fli	04/30
7 Rain	05/01
8 Flo	05/02
9 Cro	05/03
10 Wind	05/04
11 Hou	05/05
12 Liz	05/06
13 Sna	05/07
1 Dea	05/08
2 Deer	05/09
3 Rab	05/10
4 Wat	05/11
5 Dog	05/12
6 Mon	05/13
7 Gra	05/14
8 Reed	05/15
9 Jag	05/16
10 Eag	05/17
11 Vul	05/18
12 Ear	05/19
13 Fli	05/20
1 Rain	05/21
2 Flo	05/22
3 Cro	05/23
4 Wind	05/24
5 Hou	05/25
6 Liz	05/26
7 Sna	05/27
8 Dea	05/28
9 Deer	05/29
10 Rab	05/30
11 Wat	05/31
12 Dog	06/01
13 Mon	06/02
1 Gra	06/03
2 Reed	06/04

CELEBRATE NATIVE AMERICA

3 Jag	06/05	10 Reed	08/03	4 Gra	10/01	9 Wat	11/27	3 Rab	01/25	10 Deer	03/25	4 Dea	05/23	11 Sna	07/21	3 Wind	09/16	10 Cro	11/14	4 Flo	01/12	11 Rain	03/12
4 Eag	06/06	11 Jag	08/04	5 Reed	10/02	10 Dog	11/28	4 Wat	01/26	11 Rab	03/26	5 Deer	05/24	12 Dea	07/22	4 Hou	09/17	11 Wind	11/15	5 Cro	01/13	12 Flo	03/13
5 Vul	06/07	12 Eag	08/05	6 Jag	10/03	11 Mon	11/29	5 Dog	01/27	12 Wat	03/27	6 Rab	05/25	13 Deer	07/23	5 Liz	09/18	12 Hou	11/16	6 Wind	01/14	13 Cro	03/14
6 Ear	06/08	13 Vul	08/06	7 Eag	10/04	12 Gra	11/30	6 Mon	01/28	13 Dog	03/28	7 Wat	05/26	1 Rab	07/24	6 Sna	09/19	13 Liz	11/17	7 Hou	01/15	1 Wind	03/15
7 Fli	06/09	1 Ear	08/07	8 Vul	10/05	13 Reed	12/01	7 Gra	01/29	1 Mon	03/29	8 Dog	05/27	2 Wat	07/25	7 Dea	09/20	1 Sna	11/18	8 Liz	01/16	2 Hou	03/16
8 Rain	06/10	2 Fli	08/08	9 Ear	10/06	1 Jag	12/02	8 Reed	01/30	2 Gra	03/30	9 Mon	05/28	3 Dog	07/26	8 Deer	09/21	2 Dea	11/19	9 Sna	01/17	3 Liz	03/17
9 Flo	06/11	3 Rain	08/09	10 Fli	10/07	2 Eag	12/03	9 Jag	01/31	3 Reed	03/31	10 Gra	05/29	4 Mon	07/27	9 Rab	09/22	3 Rab	11/20	10 Deer	01/18	4 Sna	03/18
10 Cro	06/12	4 Flo	08/10	11 Rain	10/08	3 Vul	12/04	10 Eag	02/01	4 Jag	04/01	11 Reed	05/30	5 Gra	07/28	10 Wat	09/23	4 Rab	11/21	11 Deer	01/19	5 Dea	03/19
11 Wind	06/13	5 Cro	08/11	12 Flo	10/09	4 Ear	12/05	11 Vul	02/02	5 Eag	04/02	12 Jag	05/31	6 Reed	07/29	11 Dog	09/24	5 Wat	11/22	12 Rab	01/20	6 Deer	03/20
12 Hou	06/14	6 Wind	08/12	13 Cro	10/10	5 Fli	12/06	12 Ear	02/03	6 Vul	04/03	13 Eag	06/01	7 Jag	07/30	12 Mon	09/25	6 Dog	11/23	13 Wat	01/21	7 Rab	03/21
13 Liz	06/15	7 Hou	08/13	1 Wind	10/11	6 Rain	12/07	13 Fli	02/04	7 Ear	04/04	1 Vul	06/02	8 Eag	07/31	13 Gra	09/26	7 Mon	11/24	1 Dog	01/22	8 Wat	03/22
1 Sna	06/16	8 Liz	08/14	2 Hou	10/12	7 Flo	12/08	1 Rain	02/05	8 Fli	04/05	2 Ear	06/03	9 Vul	08/01	1 Reed	09/27	8 Gra	11/25	2 Mon	01/23	9 Dog	03/23
2 Dea	06/17	9 Sna	08/15	3 Liz	10/13	8 Cro	12/09	2 Flo	02/06	9 Rain	04/06	3 Fli	06/04	10 Ear	08/02	2 Jag	09/28	9 Reed	11/26	3 Gra	01/24	10 Mon	03/24
3 Deer	06/18	10 Dea	08/16	4 Sna	10/14	9 Wind	12/10	3 Cro	02/07	10 Flo	04/07	4 Rain	06/05	11 Fli	08/03	3 Eag	09/29	10 Jag	11/27	4 Reed	01/25	11 Gra	03/25
4 Rab	06/19	11 Deer	08/17	5 Dea	10/15	10 Hou	12/11	4 Wind	02/08	11 Cro	04/08	5 Hou	06/06	12 Rain	08/04	4 Vul	09/30	11 Eag	11/28	5 Jag	01/26	12 Reed	03/26
5 Wat	06/20	12 Rab	08/18	6 Deer	10/16	11 Liz	12/12	5 Hou	02/09	12 Wind	04/09	6 Cro	06/07	13 Flo	08/05/98	5 Ear	10/01	12 Vul	11/29	6 Eag	01/27	13 Jag	03/27
6 Dog	06/21	13 Wat	08/19	7 Rab	10/17	12 Sna	12/13	6 Liz	02/10	13 Hou	04/10	7 Wind	06/08			6 Fli	10/02	13 Ear	11/30	7 Vul	01/28	1 Eag	03/28
7 Mon	06/22	1 Dog	08/20	8 Wat	10/18	13 Dea	12/14	7 Sna	02/11	1 Liz	04/11	8 Hou	06/09	8 FLINT		7 Rain	10/03	1 Fli	12/01	8 Ear	01/29	2 Vul	03/29
8 Gra	06/23	2 Mon	08/21	9 Dog	10/19	1 Deer	12/15	8 Dea	02/12	2 Sna	04/12	9 Liz	06/10	1 Cro	08/06/98	8 Flo	10/04	2 Rain	12/02	9 Fli	01/30	3 Ear	03/30
9 Reed	06/24	3 Gra	08/22	10 Mon	10/20	2 Rab	12/16	9 Deer	02/13	3 Dea	04/13	10 Sna	06/11	2 Wind	08/07	9 Cro	10/05	3 Flo	12/03	10 Rain	01/31	4 Fli	03/31
10 Jag	06/25	4 Reed	08/23	11 Gra	10/21	3 Wat	12/17	10 Rab	02/14	4 Deer	04/14	11 Dea	06/12	3 Hou	08/08	10 Wind	10/06	4 Cro	12/04	11 Flo	02/01	5 Rain	04/01
11 Eag	06/26	5 Jag	08/24	12 Reed	10/22	4 Dog	12/18	11 Wat	02/15	5 Rab	04/15	12 Deer	06/13	4 Liz	08/09	11 Hou	10/07	5 Wind	12/05	12 Cro	02/02	6 Flo	04/02
12 Vul	06/27	6 Eag	08/25	13 Jag	10/23	5 Mon	12/19	12 Dog	02/16	6 Wat	04/16	13 Rab	06/14	5 Sna	08/10	12 Liz	10/08	6 Hou	12/06	13 Wind	02/03	7 Cro	04/03
13 Ear	06/28	7 Vul	08/26	1 Eag	10/24	6 Gra	12/20	13 Mon	02/17	7 Dog	04/17	1 Wat	06/15	6 Dea	08/11	13 Sna	10/09	7 Liz	12/07	1 Hou	02/04	8 Wind	04/04
1 Fli	06/29	8 Ear	08/27	2 Vul	10/25	7 Reed	12/21	1 Gra	02/18	8 Mon	04/18	2 Dog	06/16	7 Deer	08/12	1 Dea	10/10	8 Sna	12/08	2 Liz	02/05	9 Hou	04/05
2 Rain	06/30	9 Fli	08/28	3 Ear	10/26	8 Jag	12/22	2 Reed	02/19	9 Gra	04/19	3 Mon	06/17	8 Rab	08/13	2 Deer	10/11	9 Dea	12/09	3 Sna	02/06	10 Liz	04/06
3 Flo	07/01	10 Rain	08/29	4 Fli	10/27	9 Eag	12/23	3 Jag	02/20	10 Reed	04/20	4 Gra	06/18	9 Wat	08/14	3 Rab	10/12	10 Deer	12/10	4 Dea	02/07	11 Sna	04/07
4 Cro	07/02	11 Flo	08/30	5 Rain	10/28	10 Vul	12/24	4 Eag	02/21	11 Jag	04/21	5 Reed	06/19	10 Dog	08/15	4 Wat	10/13	11 Rab	12/11	5 Deer	02/08	12 Dea	04/08
5 Wind	07/03	12 Cro	08/31	6 Flo	10/29	11 Ear	12/25	5 Vul	02/22	12 Eag	04/22	6 Jag	06/20	11 Mon	08/16	5 Dog	10/14	12 Wat	12/12	6 Rab	02/09	13 Deer	04/09
6 Hou	07/04	13 Wind	09/01	7 Cro	10/30	12 Fli	12/26	6 Ear	02/23	13 Vul	04/23	7 Eag	06/21	12 Gra	08/17	6 Mon	10/15	13 Dog	12/13	7 Wat	02/10	1 Rab	04/10
7 Liz	07/05	1 Hou	09/02	8 Wind	10/31	13 Rain	12/27	7 Fli	02/24	1 Ear	04/24	8 Vul	06/22	13 Reed	08/18	7 Gra	10/16	1 Mon	12/14	8 Dog	02/11	2 Wat	04/11
8 Sna	07/06	2 Liz	09/03	9 Hou	11/01	1 Flo	12/28	8 Rain	02/25	2 Fli	04/25	9 Ear	06/23	1 Jag	08/19	8 Reed	10/17	2 Gra	12/15	9 Mon	02/12	3 Dog	04/12
9 Dea	07/07	3 Sna	09/04	10 Liz	11/02	2 Cro	12/29	9 Flo	02/26	3 Rain	04/26	10 Fli	06/24	2 Eag	08/20	9 Jag	10/18	3 Reed	12/16	10 Gra	02/13	4 Mon	04/13
10 Deer	07/08	4 Dea	09/05	11 Sna	11/03	3 Wind	12/30	10 Cro	02/27	4 Flo	04/27	11 Rain	06/25	3 Vul	08/21	10 Eag	10/19	4 Jag	12/17	11 Reed	02/14	5 Gra	04/14
11 Rab	07/09	5 Deer	09/06	12 Dea	11/04	4 Hou	12/31/97	11 Wind	02/28	5 Cro	04/28	12 Flo	06/26	4 Ear	08/22	11 Vul	10/20	5 Eag	12/18	12 Jag	02/15	6 Reed	04/15
12 Wat	07/10	6 Rab	09/07	13 Deer	11/05	5 Liz	01/01/98	12 Hou	03/01	6 Wind	04/29	13 Cro	06/27	5 Fli	08/23	12 Ear	10/21	6 Vul	12/19	13 Eag	02/16	7 Jag	04/16
13 Dog	07/11	7 Wat	09/08	1 Rab	11/06	6 Sna	01/02	13 Liz	03/02	7 Hou	04/30	1 Wind	06/28	6 Rain	08/24	13 Fli	10/22	7 Ear	12/20	1 Vul	02/17	8 Eag	04/17
1 Mon	07/12	8 Dog	09/09	2 Wat	11/07	7 Dea	01/03	1 Sna	03/03	8 Liz	05/01	2 Hou	06/29	7 Flo	08/25	1 Rain	10/23	8 Fli	12/21	2 Ear	02/18	9 Vul	04/18
2 Gra	07/13	9 Mon	09/10	3 Dog	11/08	8 Deer	01/04	2 Dea	03/04	9 Sna	05/02	3 Liz	06/30	8 Cro	08/26	2 Flo	10/24	9 Rain	12/22	3 Fli	02/19	10 Ear	04/19
3 Reed	07/14	10 Gra	09/11	4 Mon	11/09	9 Rab	01/05	3 Deer	03/05	10 Dea	05/03	4 Sna	07/01	9 Wind	08/27	3 Cro	10/25	10 Flo	12/23	4 Rain	02/20	11 Fli	04/20
4 Jag	07/15	11 Reed	09/12	5 Gra	11/10	10 Wat	01/06	4 Rab	03/06	11 Deer	05/04	5 Dea	07/02	10 Hou	08/28	4 Wind	10/26	11 Cro	12/24	5 Flo	02/21	12 Rain	04/21
5 Eag	07/16	12 Jag	09/13	6 Reed	11/11	11 Dog	01/07	5 Wat	03/07	12 Rab	05/05	6 Deer	07/03	11 Liz	08/29	5 Hou	10/27	12 Wind	12/25	6 Cro	02/22	13 Flo	04/22/99
6 Vul	07/17	13 Eag	09/14	7 Jag	11/12	12 Mon	01/08	6 Dog	03/08	13 Wat	05/06	7 Rab	07/04	12 Sna	08/30	6 Liz	10/28	13 Hou	12/26	7 Wind	02/23		
7 Ear	07/18	1 Vul	09/15	8 Eag	11/13	13 Gra	01/09	7 Mon	03/09	1 Dog	05/07	8 Wat	07/05	13 Dea	08/31	7 Sna	10/29	1 Liz	12/27	8 Hou	02/24	9 HOUSE	
8 Fli	07/19	2 Ear	09/16	9 Vul	11/14	1 Reed	01/10	8 Gra	03/10	2 Mon	05/08	9 Dog	07/06	1 Deer	09/01	8 Dea	10/30	2 Sna	12/28	9 Liz	02/25	1 Cro	04/23/99
9 Rain	07/20	3 Fli	09/17	10 Ear	11/15	2 Jag	01/11	9 Reed	03/11	3 Gra	05/09	10 Mon	07/07	2 Rab	09/02	9 Deer	10/31	3 Dea	12/29	10 Sna	02/26	2 Wind	04/24
10 Flo	07/21	4 Rain	09/18	11 Fli	11/16	3 Eag	01/12	10 Jag	03/12	4 Reed	05/10	11 Gra	07/08	3 Wat	09/03	10 Rab	11/01	4 Deer	12/30	11 Dea	02/27	3 Hou	04/25
11 Cro	07/22	5 Flo	09/19	12 Rain	11/17	4 Vul	01/13	11 Eag	03/13	5 Jag	05/11	12 Reed	07/09	4 Dog	09/04	11 Wat	11/02	5 Rab	12/31/98	12 Deer	02/28	4 Liz	04/26
12 Wind	07/23	6 Cro	09/20	13 Flo	11/18/97	5 Ear	01/14	12 Vul	03/14	6 Eag	05/12	13 Jag	07/10	5 Mon	09/05	12 Dog	11/03	6 Wat	01/01/99	13 Rab	03/01	5 Sna	04/27
13 Hou	07/24	7 Wind	09/21			6 Fli	01/15	13 Ear	03/15	7 Vul	05/13	1 Eag	07/11	6 Gra	09/06	13 Mon	11/04	7 Dog	01/02	1 Wat	03/02	6 Dea	04/28
1 Liz	07/25	8 Hou	09/22	7 REED		7 Rain	01/16	1 Fli	03/16	8 Ear	05/14	2 Vul	07/12	7 Reed	09/07	1 Gra	11/05	8 Mon	01/03	2 Dog	03/03	7 Deer	04/29
2 Sna	07/26	9 Liz	09/23	1 Cro	11/19/97	8 Flo	01/17	2 Rain	03/17	9 Fli	05/15	3 Ear	07/13	8 Jag	09/08	2 Reed	11/06	9 Gra	01/04	3 Mon	03/04	8 Rab	04/30
3 Dea	07/27	10 Sna	09/24	2 Wind	11/20	9 Cro	01/18	3 Flo	03/18	10 Rain	05/16	4 Fli	07/14	9 Eag	09/09	3 Jag	11/07	10 Reed	01/05	4 Gra	03/05	9 Wat	05/01
4 Deer	07/28	11 Dea	09/25	3 Hou	11/21	10 Wind	01/19	4 Cro	03/19	11 Flo	05/17	5 Rain	07/15	10 Vul	09/10	4 Eag	11/08	11 Jag	01/06	5 Reed	03/06	10 Dog	05/02
5 Rab	07/29	12 Deer	09/26	4 Liz	11/22	11 Hou	01/20	5 Wind	03/20	12 Cro	05/18	6 Flo	07/16	11 Ear	09/11	5 Vul	11/09	12 Eag	01/07	6 Jag	03/07	11 Mon	05/03
6 Wat	07/30	13 Rab	09/27	5 Sna	11/23	12 Liz	01/21	6 Hou	03/21	13 Wind	05/19	7 Cro	07/17	12 Fli	09/12	6 Ear	11/10	13 Vul	01/08	7 Eag	03/08	12 Gra	05/04
7 Dog	07/31	1 Wat	09/28	6 Dea	11/24	13 Sna	01/22	1 Hou	05/20			8 Wind	07/18	13 Rain	09/13	7 Fli	11/11	1 Ear	01/09	8 Vul	03/09	13 Reed	05/05
8 Mon	08/01	2 Dog	09/29	7 Deer	11/25	1 Dea	01/23	2 Liz	05/21			9 Hou	07/19	1 Flo	09/14	8 Rain	11/12	2 Fli	01/10	9 Ear	03/10	1 Jag	05/06
9 Gra	08/02	3 Mon	09/30	8 Rab	11/26	2 Deer	01/24	3 Sna	05/22			10 Liz	07/20	2 Cro	09/15	9 Flo	11/13	3 Rain	01/11	10 Fli	03/11	2 Eag	05/07

64

CONCORDANCE TABLES

#	Day	Date	#	Day	Date	#	Day	Date	#	Day	Date	#	Day	Date	#	Day	Date	#	Day	Date	#	Day	Date	#	Day	Date	#	Day	Date	#	Day	Date	#	Day	Date	#	Day	Date
3	Vul	05/08	10	Eag	07/06	4	Jag	09/03	11	Reed	11/01	5	Gra	12/30	10	Wat	02/25	4	Rab	04/24	11	Deer	06/22	5	Dea	08/20	10	Hou	10/16	4	Wind	12/14	11	Cro	02/11
4	Ear	05/09	11	Vul	07/07	5	Eag	09/04	12	Jag	11/02	6	Reed	12/31/99	11	Dog	02/26	5	Wat	04/25	12	Rab	06/23	6	Deer	08/21	11	Liz	10/17	5	Hou	12/15	12	Wind	02/12
5	Fli	05/10	12	Ear	07/08	6	Vul	09/05	13	Jag	11/03	7	Jag	01/01/00	12	Mon	02/27	6	Dog	04/26	13	Wat	06/24	7	Rab	08/22	12	Sna	10/18	6	Liz	12/16	13	Hou	02/13
6	Rain	05/11	13	Fli	07/09	7	Ear	09/06	1	Vul	11/04	8	Eag	01/02	13	Gra	02/28	7	Mon	04/27	1	Dog	06/25	8	Wat	08/23	13	Dea	10/19	7	Sna	12/17	1	Liz	02/14
7	Flo	05/12	1	Rain	07/10	8	Fli	09/07	2	Ear	11/05	9	Vul	01/03	1	Reed	02/29	8	Gra	04/28	2	Mon	06/26	9	Dog	08/24	1	Deer	10/20	8	Dea	12/18	2	Sna	02/15
8	Cro	05/13	2	Flo	07/11	9	Rain	09/08	3	Fli	11/06	10	Ear	01/04	2	Jag	03/01	9	Reed	04/29	3	Gra	06/27	10	Mon	08/25	2	Rab	10/21	9	Deer	12/19	3	Dea	02/16
9	Wind	05/14	3	Cro	07/12	10	Flo	09/09	4	Rain	11/07	11	Fli	01/05	3	Eag	03/02	10	Jag	04/30	4	Reed	06/28	11	Gra	08/26	3	Wat	10/22	10	Rab	12/20	4	Deer	02/17
10	Hou	05/15	4	Wind	07/13	11	Cro	09/10	5	Flo	11/08	12	Rain	01/06	4	Vul	03/03	11	Eag	05/01	5	Jag	06/29	12	Reed	08/27	4	Dog	10/23	11	Wat	12/21	5	Rab	02/18
11	Liz	05/16	5	Hou	07/14	12	Wind	09/11	6	Cro	11/09	13	Flo	01/07/00	5	Ear	03/04	12	Vul	05/02	6	Eag	06/30	13	Jag	08/28	5	Mon	10/24	12	Dog	12/22	6	Wat	02/19
12	Sna	05/17	6	Liz	07/15	13	Hou	09/12	7	Wind	11/10				6	Fli	03/05	13	Ear	05/03	7	Vul	07/01	1	Eag	08/29	6	Gra	10/25	13	Mon	12/23	7	Dog	02/20
13	Dea	05/18	7	Sna	07/16	1	Liz	09/13	8	Hou	11/11		10 RABBIT		7	Rain	03/06	1	Fli	05/04	8	Ear	07/02	2	Vul	08/30	7	Reed	10/26	1	Gra	12/24	8	Mon	02/21
1	Deer	05/19	8	Dea	07/17	2	Sna	09/14	9	Liz	11/12	1	Cro	01/08/00	8	Flo	03/07	2	Rain	05/05	9	Fli	07/03	3	Ear	08/31	8	Jag	10/27	2	Reed	12/25	9	Gra	02/22
2	Rab	05/20	9	Deer	07/18	3	Dea	09/15	10	Sna	11/13	2	Wind	01/09	9	Cro	03/08	3	Flo	05/06	10	Rain	07/04	4	Fli	09/01	9	Eag	10/28	3	Jag	12/26	10	Reed	02/23
3	Wat	05/21	10	Rab	07/19	4	Deer	09/16	11	Dea	11/14	3	Hou	01/10	10	Wind	03/09	4	Cro	05/07	11	Flo	07/05	5	Rain	09/02	10	Vul	10/29	4	Eag	12/27	11	Jag	02/24
4	Dog	05/22	11	Wat	07/20	5	Rab	09/17	12	Deer	11/15	4	Liz	01/11	11	Hou	03/10	5	Wind	05/08	12	Cro	07/06	6	Flo	09/03	11	Ear	10/30	5	Vul	12/28	12	Eag	02/25
5	Mon	05/23	12	Dog	07/21	6	Wat	09/18	13	Rab	11/16	5	Sna	01/12	12	Liz	03/11	6	Hou	05/09	13	Wind	07/07	7	Cro	09/04	12	Fli	10/31	6	Ear	12/29	13	Vul	02/26
6	Gra	05/24	13	Mon	07/22	7	Dog	09/19	1	Wat	11/17	6	Dea	01/13	13	Sna	03/12	7	Liz	05/10	1	Hou	07/08	8	Wind	09/05	13	Rain	11/01	7	Fli	12/30	1	Ear	02/27
7	Reed	05/25	1	Gra	07/23	8	Mon	09/20	2	Dog	11/18	7	Deer	01/14	1	Dea	03/13	8	Sna	05/11	2	Liz	07/09	9	Hou	09/06	1	Flo	11/02	8	Rain	12/31/00	2	Fli	02/28
8	Jag	05/26	2	Reed	07/24	9	Gra	09/21	3	Mon	11/19	8	Rab	01/15	2	Deer	03/14	9	Dea	05/12	3	Sna	07/10	10	Liz	09/07	2	Cro	11/03	9	Flo	01/01/01	3	Rain	03/01
9	Eag	05/27	3	Jag	07/25	10	Reed	09/22	4	Gra	11/20	9	Wat	01/16	3	Rab	03/15	10	Deer	05/13	4	Dea	07/11	11	Sna	09/08	3	Wind	11/04	10	Cro	01/02	4	Flo	03/02
10	Vul	05/28	4	Eag	07/26	11	Jag	09/23	5	Reed	11/21	10	Dog	01/17	4	Wat	03/16	11	Rab	05/14	5	Deer	07/12	12	Dea	09/09	4	Hou	11/05	11	Wind	01/03	5	Cro	03/03
11	Ear	05/29	5	Vul	07/27	12	Eag	09/24	6	Jag	11/22	11	Mon	01/18	5	Dog	03/17	12	Wat	05/15	6	Rab	07/13	13	Deer	09/10	5	Liz	11/06	12	Hou	01/04	6	Wind	03/04
12	Fli	05/30	6	Ear	07/28	13	Vul	09/25	7	Eag	11/23	12	Gra	01/19	6	Mon	03/18	13	Dog	05/16	7	Wat	07/14	1	Rab	09/11	6	Sna	11/07	13	Liz	01/05	7	Hou	03/05
13	Rain	05/31	7	Fli	07/29	1	Ear	09/26	8	Vul	11/24	13	Reed	01/20	7	Gra	03/19	1	Mon	05/17	8	Deer	07/15	2	Wat	09/12	7	Dea	11/08	1	Sna	01/06	8	Liz	03/06
1	Flo	06/01	8	Rain	07/30	2	Fli	09/27	9	Ear	11/25	1	Jag	01/21	8	Reed	03/20	2	Gra	05/18	9	Jag	07/16	3	Dog	09/13	8	Deer	11/09	2	Dea	01/07	9	Sna	03/07
2	Cro	06/02	9	Flo	07/31	3	Rain	09/28	10	Fli	11/26	2	Eag	01/22	9	Jag	03/21	3	Reed	05/19	10	Gra	07/17	4	Mon	09/14	9	Rab	11/10	3	Deer	01/08	10	Dea	03/08
3	Wind	06/03	10	Cro	08/01	4	Flo	09/29	11	Rain	11/27	3	Vul	01/23	10	Eag	03/22	4	Jag	05/20	11	Reed	07/18	5	Gra	09/15	10	Wat	11/11	4	Rab	01/09	11	Deer	03/09
4	Hou	06/04	11	Wind	08/02	5	Cro	09/30	12	Flo	11/28	4	Ear	01/24	11	Vul	03/23	5	Eag	05/21	12	Jag	07/19	6	Reed	09/16	11	Dog	11/12	5	Wat	01/10	12	Rab	03/10
5	Liz	06/05	12	Hou	08/03	6	Wind	10/01	13	Cro	11/29	5	Fli	01/25	12	Ear	03/24	6	Vul	05/22	13	Eag	07/20	7	Jag	09/17	12	Mon	11/13	6	Dog	01/11	13	Wat	03/11
6	Sna	06/06	13	Liz	08/04	7	Hou	10/02	1	Wind	11/30	6	Rain	01/26	13	Fli	03/25	7	Ear	05/23	1	Vul	07/21	8	Eag	09/18	13	Gra	11/14	7	Mon	01/12	1	Dog	03/12
7	Dea	06/07	1	Sna	08/05	8	Liz	10/03	2	Hou	12/01	7	Flo	01/27	1	Rain	03/26	8	Fli	05/24	2	Ear	07/22	9	Vul	09/19	1	Reed	11/15	8	Gra	01/13	2	Mon	03/13
8	Deer	06/08	2	Dea	08/06	9	Sna	10/04	3	Liz	12/02	8	Cro	01/28	2	Flo	03/27	9	Rain	05/25	3	Fli	07/23	10	Ear	09/20	2	Jag	11/16	9	Reed	01/14	3	Gra	03/14
9	Rab	06/09	3	Deer	08/07	10	Dea	10/05	4	Sna	12/03	9	Wind	01/29	3	Cro	03/28	10	Flo	05/26	4	Rain	07/24	11	Fli	09/21	3	Eag	11/17	10	Jag	01/15	4	Reed	03/15
10	Wat	06/10	4	Rab	08/08	11	Deer	10/06	5	Dea	12/04	10	Hou	01/30	4	Wind	03/29	11	Cro	05/27	5	Flo	07/25	12	Rain	09/22	4	Vul	11/18	11	Eag	01/16	5	Jag	03/16
11	Dog	06/11	5	Wat	08/09	12	Rab	10/07	6	Deer	12/05	11	Liz	01/31	5	Hou	03/30	12	Wind	05/28	6	Cro	07/26	13	Flo	09/23/00	5	Ear	11/19	12	Vul	01/17	6	Eag	03/17
12	Mon	06/12	6	Dog	08/10	13	Wat	10/08	7	Rab	12/06	12	Sna	02/01	6	Liz	03/31	13	Hou	05/29	7	Wind	07/27				6	Fli	11/20	13	Ear	01/18	7	Vul	03/18
13	Gra	06/13	7	Mon	08/11	1	Dog	10/09	8	Wat	12/07	13	Dea	02/02	7	Sna	04/01	1	Liz	05/30	8	Hou	07/28		11 REED		7	Rain	11/21	1	Fli	01/19	8	Ear	03/19
1	Reed	06/14	8	Gra	08/12	2	Mon	10/10	9	Dog	12/08	1	Deer	02/03	8	Dea	04/02	2	Sna	05/31	9	Liz	07/29	1	Cro	09/24/00	8	Flo	11/22	2	Rain	01/20	9	Fli	03/20
2	Jag	06/15	9	Reed	08/13	3	Gra	10/11	10	Mon	12/09	2	Rab	02/04	9	Deer	04/03	3	Dea	06/01	10	Sna	07/30	2	Wind	09/25	9	Cro	11/23	3	Flo	01/21	10	Rain	03/21
3	Eag	06/16	10	Jag	08/14	4	Reed	10/12	11	Gra	12/10	3	Wat	02/05	10	Rab	04/04	4	Deer	06/02	11	Dea	07/31	3	Hou	09/26	10	Wind	11/24	4	Cro	01/22	11	Flo	03/22
4	Vul	06/17	11	Eag	08/15	5	Jag	10/13	12	Reed	12/11	4	Dog	02/06	11	Wat	04/05	5	Rab	06/03	12	Deer	08/01	4	Liz	09/27	11	Hou	11/25	5	Wind	01/23	12	Cro	03/23
5	Ear	06/18	12	Vul	08/16	6	Eag	10/14	13	Jag	12/12	5	Mon	02/07	12	Dog	04/06	6	Wat	06/04	13	Rab	08/02	5	Sna	09/28	12	Liz	11/26	6	Hou	01/24	13	Wind	03/24
6	Fli	06/19	13	Ear	08/17	7	Vul	10/15	1	Eag	12/13	6	Gra	02/08	13	Mon	04/07	7	Dog	06/05	1	Wat	08/03	6	Dea	09/29	13	Sna	11/27	7	Liz	01/25	1	Hou	03/25
7	Rain	06/20	1	Fli	08/18	8	Ear	10/16	2	Vul	12/14	7	Reed	02/09	1	Gra	04/08	8	Mon	06/06	2	Dog	08/04	7	Deer	09/30	1	Dea	11/28	8	Sna	01/26	2	Liz	03/26
8	Flo	06/21	2	Rain	08/19	9	Fli	10/17	3	Ear	12/15	8	Jag	02/10	2	Reed	04/09	9	Gra	06/07	3	Mon	08/05	8	Rab	10/01	2	Deer	11/29	9	Dea	01/27	3	Sna	03/27
9	Cro	06/22	3	Flo	08/20	10	Rain	10/18	4	Fli	12/16	9	Eag	02/11	3	Jag	04/10	10	Reed	06/08	4	Gra	08/06	9	Wat	10/02	3	Rab	11/30	10	Deer	01/28	4	Dea	03/28
10	Wind	06/23	4	Cro	08/21	11	Flo	10/19	5	Rain	12/17	10	Vul	02/12	4	Eag	04/11	11	Jag	06/09	5	Reed	08/07	10	Dog	10/03	4	Wat	12/01	11	Rab	01/29	5	Deer	03/29
11	Hou	06/24	5	Wind	08/22	12	Cro	10/20	6	Flo	12/18	11	Ear	02/13	5	Vul	04/12	12	Eag	06/10	6	Jag	08/08	11	Mon	10/04	5	Dog	12/02	12	Wat	01/30	6	Rab	03/30
12	Liz	06/25	6	Hou	08/23	13	Wind	10/21	7	Cro	12/19	12	Fli	02/14	6	Ear	04/13	13	Vul	06/11	7	Eag	08/09	12	Gra	10/05	6	Mon	12/03	13	Dog	01/31	7	Wat	03/31
13	Sna	06/26	7	Liz	08/24	1	Hou	10/22	8	Wind	12/20	13	Rain	02/15	7	Fli	04/14	1	Ear	06/12	8	Vul	08/10	13	Reed	10/06	7	Gra	12/04	1	Mon	02/01	8	Dog	04/01
1	Dea	06/27	8	Sna	08/25	2	Liz	10/23	9	Hou	12/21	1	Flo	02/16	8	Rain	04/15	2	Fli	06/13	9	Ear	08/11	1	Jag	10/07	8	Reed	12/05	2	Gra	02/02	9	Mon	04/02
2	Deer	06/28	9	Dea	08/26	3	Sna	10/24	10	Liz	12/22	2	Cro	02/17	9	Flo	04/16	3	Rain	06/14	10	Fli	08/12	2	Eag	10/08	9	Jag	12/06	3	Reed	02/03	10	Gra	04/03
3	Rab	06/29	10	Deer	08/27	4	Dea	10/25	11	Sna	12/23	3	Wind	02/18	10	Cro	04/17	4	Flo	06/15	11	Rain	08/13	3	Vul	10/09	10	Eag	12/07	4	Jag	02/04	11	Reed	04/04
4	Wat	06/30	11	Rab	08/28	5	Deer	10/26	12	Dea	12/24	4	Hou	02/19	11	Wind	04/18	5	Cro	06/16	12	Flo	08/14	4	Ear	10/10	11	Vul	12/08	5	Eag	02/05	12	Jag	04/05
5	Dog	07/01	12	Wat	08/29	6	Rab	10/27	13	Deer	12/25	5	Liz	02/20	12	Hou	04/19	6	Wind	06/17	13	Cro	08/15	5	Fli	10/11	12	Ear	12/09	6	Vul	02/06	13	Eag	04/06
6	Mon	07/02	13	Dog	08/30	7	Wat	10/28	1	Rab	12/26	6	Sna	02/21	13	Liz	04/20	7	Hou	06/18	1	Wind	08/16	6	Rain	10/12	13	Fli	12/10	7	Ear	02/07	1	Vul	04/07
7	Gra	07/03	1	Mon	08/31	8	Dog	10/29	2	Wat	12/27	7	Dea	02/22	1	Sna	04/21	8	Liz	06/19	2	Hou	08/17	7	Flo	10/13	1	Rain	12/11	8	Fli	02/08	2	Ear	04/08
8	Reed	07/04	2	Gra	09/01	9	Mon	10/30	3	Dog	12/28	8	Deer	02/23	2	Dea	04/22	9	Sna	06/20	3	Liz	08/18	8	Cro	10/14	2	Flo	12/12	9	Rain	02/09	3	Fli	04/09
9	Jag	07/05	3	Reed	09/02	10	Gra	10/31	4	Mon	12/29	9	Rab	02/24	3	Deer	04/23	10	Dea	06/21	4	Sna	08/19	9	Wind	10/15	3	Cro	12/13	10	Flo	02/10	4	Rain	04/10

65

CELEBRATE NATIVE AMERICA

5 Flo	04/11	12 Rain	06/09	4 Vul	08/05	11 Eag	10/03	5 Jag	12/01	12 Reed	01/29	4 Dog	03/27	11 Wat	05/25	5 Rab	07/23	12 Deer	09/20
6 Cro	04/12	13 Flo	06/10/01	5 Ear	08/06	12 Vul	10/04	6 Eag	12/02	13 Jag	01/30	5 Mon	03/28	12 Dog	05/26	6 Wat	07/24	13 Rab	09/21
7 Wind	04/13			6 Fli	08/07	13 Ear	10/05	7 Vul	12/03	1 Eag	01/31	6 Gra	03/29	13 Mon	05/27	7 Dog	07/25	1 Wat	09/22
8 Hou	04/14	12 FLINT		7 Rain	08/08	1 Fli	10/06	8 Ear	12/04	2 Vul	02/01	7 Reed	03/30	1 Gra	05/28	8 Mon	07/26	2 Dog	09/23
9 Liz	04/15	1 Cro	06/11/01	8 Flo	08/09	2 Rain	10/07	9 Fli	12/05	3 Ear	02/02	8 Jag	03/31	2 Reed	05/29	9 Gra	07/27	3 Mon	09/24
10 Sna	04/16	2 Wind	06/12	9 Cro	08/10	3 Flo	10/08	10 Rain	12/06	4 Fli	02/03	9 Eag	04/01	3 Jag	05/30	10 Reed	07/28	4 Gra	09/25
11 Dea	04/17	3 Hou	06/13	10 Wind	08/11	4 Cro	10/09	11 Flo	12/07	5 Rain	02/04	10 Vul	04/02	4 Eag	05/31	11 Jag	07/29	5 Reed	09/26
12 Deer	04/18	4 Liz	06/14	11 Hou	08/12	5 Wind	10/10	12 Cro	12/08	6 Flo	02/05	11 Ear	04/03	5 Vul	06/01	12 Eag	07/30	6 Jag	09/27
13 Rab	04/19	5 Sna	06/15	12 Liz	08/13	6 Hou	10/11	13 Wind	12/09	7 Cro	02/06	12 Fli	04/04	6 Ear	06/02	13 Vul	07/31	7 Eag	09/28
1 Wat	04/20	6 Dea	06/16	13 Sna	08/14	7 Liz	10/12	1 Hou	12/10	8 Wind	02/07	13 Rain	04/05	7 Fli	06/03	1 Ear	08/01	8 Vul	09/29
2 Dog	04/21	7 Deer	06/17	1 Dea	08/15	8 Sna	10/13	2 Liz	12/11	9 Hou	02/08	1 Flo	04/06	8 Rain	06/04	2 Fli	08/02	9 Ear	09/30
3 Mon	04/22	8 Rab	06/18	2 Deer	08/16	9 Dea	10/14	3 Sna	12/12	10 Liz	02/09	2 Cro	04/07	9 Flo	06/05	3 Rain	08/03	10 Fli	10/01
4 Gra	04/23	9 Wat	06/19	3 Rab	08/17	10 Deer	10/15	4 Dea	12/13	11 Sna	02/10	3 Wind	04/08	10 Cro	06/06	4 Flo	08/04	11 Rain	10/02
5 Reed	04/24	10 Dog	06/20	4 Wat	08/18	11 Rab	10/16	5 Deer	12/14	12 Dea	02/11	4 Hou	04/09	11 Wind	06/07	5 Cro	08/05	12 Flo	10/03
6 Jag	04/25	11 Mon	06/21	5 Dog	08/19	12 Wat	10/17	6 Rab	12/15	13 Deer	02/12	5 Liz	04/10	12 Hou	06/08	6 Wind	08/06	13 Cro	10/04
7 Eag	04/26	12 Gra	06/22	6 Mon	08/20	13 Dog	10/18	7 Wat	12/16	1 Rab	02/13	6 Sna	04/11	13 Liz	06/09	7 Hou	08/07	1 Wind	10/05
8 Vul	04/27	13 Reed	06/23	7 Gra	08/21	1 Mon	10/19	8 Dog	12/17	2 Wat	02/14	7 Dea	04/12	1 Sna	06/10	8 Liz	08/08	2 Hou	10/06
9 Ear	04/28	1 Jag	06/24	8 Reed	08/22	2 Gra	10/20	9 Mon	12/18	3 Dog	02/15	8 Deer	04/13	2 Dea	06/11	9 Sna	08/09	3 Liz	10/07
10 Fli	04/29	2 Eag	06/25	9 Jag	08/23	3 Reed	10/21	10 Gra	12/19	4 Mon	02/16	9 Rab	04/14	3 Deer	06/12	10 Dea	08/10	4 Sna	10/08
11 Rain	04/30	3 Vul	06/26	10 Eag	08/24	4 Jag	10/22	11 Reed	12/20	5 Gra	02/17	10 Wat	04/15	4 Rab	06/13	11 Deer	08/11	5 Dea	10/09
12 Flo	05/01	4 Ear	06/27	11 Vul	08/25	5 Eag	10/23	12 Jag	12/21	6 Reed	02/18	11 Dog	04/16	5 Wat	06/14	12 Rab	08/12	6 Deer	10/10
13 Cro	05/02	5 Fli	06/28	12 Ear	08/26	6 Vul	10/24	13 Eag	12/22	7 Jag	02/19	12 Mon	04/17	6 Dog	06/15	13 Wat	08/13	7 Rab	10/11
1 Wind	05/03	6 Rain	06/29	13 Fli	08/27	7 Ear	10/25	1 Vul	12/23	8 Eag	02/20	13 Gra	04/18	7 Mon	06/16	1 Dog	08/14	8 Wat	10/12
2 Hou	05/04	7 Flo	06/30	1 Rain	08/28	8 Fli	10/26	2 Ear	12/24	9 Vul	02/21	1 Reed	04/19	8 Gra	06/17	2 Mon	08/15	9 Dog	10/13
3 Liz	05/05	8 Cro	07/01	2 Flo	08/29	9 Rain	10/27	3 Fli	12/25	10 Ear	02/22	2 Jag	04/20	9 Reed	06/18	3 Gra	08/16	10 Mon	10/14
4 Sna	05/06	9 Wind	07/02	3 Cro	08/30	10 Flo	10/28	4 Rain	12/26	11 Fli	02/23	3 Eag	04/21	10 Jag	06/19	4 Reed	08/17	11 Gra	10/15
5 Dea	05/07	10 Hou	07/03	4 Wind	08/31	11 Cro	10/29	5 Flo	12/27	12 Rain	02/24	4 Vul	04/22	11 Eag	06/20	5 Jag	08/18	12 Reed	10/16
6 Deer	05/08	11 Liz	07/04	5 Hou	09/01	12 Wind	10/30	6 Cro	12/28	13 Flo	02/25/02	5 Ear	04/23	12 Vul	06/21	6 Eag	08/19	13 Jag	10/17
7 Rab	05/09	12 Sna	07/05	6 Liz	09/02	13 Hou	10/31	7 Wind	12/29			6 Fli	04/24	13 Ear	06/22	7 Vul	08/20	1 Eag	10/18
8 Wat	05/10	13 Dea	07/06	7 Sna	09/03	1 Liz	11/01	8 Hou	12/30	13 HOUSE		7 Rain	04/25	1 Fli	06/23	8 Ear	08/21	2 Vul	10/19
9 Dog	05/11	1 Deer	07/07	8 Dea	09/04	2 Sna	11/02	9 Liz	12/31/01	1 Cro	02/26/02	8 Flo	04/26	2 Rain	06/24	9 Fli	08/22	3 Ear	10/20
10 Mon	05/12	2 Rab	07/08	9 Deer	09/05	3 Dea	11/03	10 Sna	01/01/02	2 Wind	02/27	9 Cro	04/27	3 Flo	06/25	10 Rain	08/23	4 Fli	10/21
11 Gra	05/13	3 Wat	07/09	10 Rab	09/06	4 Deer	11/04	11 Dea	01/02	3 Hou	02/28	10 Wind	04/28	4 Cro	06/26	11 Flo	08/24	5 Rain	10/22
12 Reed	05/14	4 Dog	07/10	11 Wat	09/07	5 Rab	11/05	12 Deer	01/03	4 Liz	03/01	11 Hou	04/29	5 Wind	06/27	12 Cro	08/25	6 Flo	10/23
13 Jag	05/15	5 Mon	07/11	12 Dog	09/08	6 Wat	11/06	13 Rab	01/04	5 Sna	03/02	12 Liz	04/30	6 Hou	06/28	13 Wind	08/26	7 Cro	10/24
1 Eag	05/16	6 Gra	07/12	13 Mon	09/09	7 Dog	11/07	1 Wat	01/05	6 Dea	03/03	13 Sna	05/01	7 Liz	06/29	1 Hou	08/27	8 Wind	10/25
2 Vul	05/17	7 Reed	07/13	1 Gra	09/10	8 Mon	11/08	2 Dog	01/06	7 Deer	03/04	1 Dea	05/02	8 Sna	06/30	2 Liz	08/28	9 Hou	10/26
3 Ear	05/18	8 Jag	07/14	2 Reed	09/11	9 Gra	11/09	3 Mon	01/07	8 Rab	03/05	2 Deer	05/03	9 Dea	07/01	3 Sna	08/29	10 Liz	10/27
4 Fli	05/19	9 Eag	07/15	3 Jag	09/12	10 Reed	11/10	4 Gra	01/08	9 Wat	03/06	3 Rab	05/04	10 Deer	07/02	4 Dea	08/30	11 Sna	10/28
5 Rain	05/20	10 Vul	07/16	4 Eag	09/13	11 Jag	11/11	5 Reed	01/09	10 Dog	03/07	4 Wat	05/05	11 Rab	07/03	5 Deer	08/31	12 Dea	10/29
6 Flo	05/21	11 Ear	07/17	5 Vul	09/14	12 Eag	11/12	6 Jag	01/10	11 Mon	03/08	5 Dog	05/06	12 Wat	07/04	6 Rab	09/01	13 Deer	10/30
7 Cro	05/22	12 Fli	07/18	6 Ear	09/15	13 Vul	11/13	7 Eag	01/11	12 Gra	03/09	6 Mon	05/07	13 Dog	07/05	7 Wat	09/02	1 Rab	10/31
8 Wind	05/23	13 Rain	07/19	7 Fli	09/16	1 Ear	11/14	8 Vul	01/12	13 Reed	03/10	7 Gra	05/08	1 Mon	07/06	8 Dog	09/03	2 Wat	11/01
9 Hou	05/24	1 Flo	07/20	8 Rain	09/17	2 Fli	11/15	9 Ear	01/13	1 Jag	03/11	8 Reed	05/09	2 Gra	07/07	9 Mon	09/04	3 Dog	11/02
10 Liz	05/25	2 Cro	07/21	9 Flo	09/18	3 Rain	11/16	10 Fli	01/14	2 Eag	03/12	9 Jag	05/10	3 Reed	07/08	10 Gra	09/05	4 Mon	11/03
11 Sna	05/26	3 Wind	07/22	10 Cro	09/19	4 Flo	11/17	11 Rain	01/15	3 Vul	03/13	10 Eag	05/11	4 Jag	07/09	11 Reed	09/06	5 Gra	11/04
12 Dea	05/27	4 Hou	07/23	11 Wind	09/20	5 Cro	11/18	12 Flo	01/16	4 Ear	03/14	11 Vul	05/12	5 Eag	07/10	12 Jag	09/07	6 Reed	11/05
13 Deer	05/28	5 Liz	07/24	12 Hou	09/21	6 Wind	11/19	13 Cro	01/17	5 Fli	03/15	12 Ear	05/13	6 Vul	07/11	13 Eag	09/08	7 Jag	11/06
1 Rab	05/29	6 Sna	07/25	13 Liz	09/22	7 Hou	11/20	1 Wind	01/18	6 Rain	03/16	13 Fli	05/14	7 Ear	07/12	1 Vul	09/09	8 Eag	11/07
2 Wat	05/30	7 Dea	07/26	1 Sna	09/23	8 Liz	11/21	2 Hou	01/19	7 Flo	03/17	1 Rain	05/15	8 Fli	07/13	2 Ear	09/10	9 Vul	11/08
3 Dog	05/31	8 Deer	07/27	2 Dea	09/24	9 Sna	11/22	3 Liz	01/20	8 Cro	03/18	2 Flo	05/16	9 Rain	07/14	3 Fli	09/11	10 Ear	11/09
4 Mon	06/01	9 Rab	07/28	3 Deer	09/25	10 Dea	11/23	4 Sna	01/21	9 Wind	03/19	3 Cro	05/17	10 Flo	07/15	4 Rain	09/12	11 Fli	11/10
5 Gra	06/02	10 Wat	07/29	4 Rab	09/26	11 Deer	11/24	5 Dea	01/22	10 Hou	03/20	4 Wind	05/18	11 Cro	07/16	5 Flo	09/13	12 Rain	11/11
6 Reed	06/03	11 Dog	07/30	5 Wat	09/27	12 Rab	11/25	6 Deer	01/23	11 Liz	03/21	5 Hou	05/19	12 Wind	07/17	6 Cro	09/14	13 Flo	11/12/02
7 Jag	06/04	12 Mon	07/31	6 Dog	09/28	13 Wat	11/26	7 Rab	01/24	12 Sna	03/22	6 Liz	05/20	13 Hou	07/18	7 Wind	09/15		
8 Eag	06/05	13 Gra	08/01	7 Mon	09/29	1 Dog	11/27	8 Wat	01/25	13 Dea	03/23	7 Sna	05/21	1 Liz	07/19	8 Hou	09/16		
9 Vul	06/06	1 Reed	08/02	8 Gra	09/30	2 Mon	11/28	9 Dog	01/26	1 Deer	03/24	8 Dea	05/22	2 Sna	07/20	9 Liz	09/17		
10 Ear	06/07	2 Jag	08/03	9 Reed	10/01	3 Gra	11/29	10 Mon	01/27	2 Rab	03/25	9 Deer	05/23	3 Dea	07/21	10 Sna	09/18		
11 Fli	06/08	3 Eag	08/04	10 Jag	10/02	4 Reed	11/30	11 Gra	01/28	3 Wat	03/26	10 Rab	05/24	4 Deer	07/22	11 Dea	09/19		

SOURCES

I. The Aztec codices used in preparing the designs of this Tonalamatl are the following:

Codex Borbonicus, in the Bibliotheque de la Palais Bourbon, Paris, contains a tonalamatl, lists of festivals, and the cycle of years. Edition E. T. Hamy (Paris, 1899).

Codex Borgia, in the Vatican Library, may have originated in Texcoco. It includes creation legends, a tonalamatl, and material on the relationship between Tlaloc and maize and is dedicated to Tezcatlipoca. Edition Fondo de Cultura Economica Mexico, 1963.

Codex Fejervary-Mayer, in the Liverpool City Museum, is a tonalamatl with much unexplained material and is again dedicated to Tezcatlipoca. Edition Duc de Loubat, Paris, 1901.

Codex Magliabecchi, prepared for the first mayor of Mexico City, Cervantes de Salazar, contains information on the gods, ceremonies, and a tonalamatl. The original is in Madrid. Partial edition Duc de Loubat, Rome, 1904.

Codex Nuttall (Zouche manuscript), in the British Museum, on one side is a Mixtec dynastic history from the mid-seventh to the mid-fourteenth centuries. On the other it is a history of the hero Eight Deer, a lord of the city of Tilantongo in the eleventh century also known as Jaguar Claw.

Codex Vaticanus, in the Vatican Library, is also a tonalamatl and is dedicated to Macuilxochitl. Edition Duc de Loubat, Rome, 1896.

II. The following is a list of the other surviving Aztec codices (which were not influential in the designs):

Codex Aubin, in the Bibliotheque Nationale, Paris, is a tonalamatl in late Aztec style. Edition Duc de Loubat, Berlin, 1901.

Codex Becker I and *Codex Becker II*, in the Museum fur Volkerkunde, Vienna, are short Mixtec dynastic histories. Edition K. A. Nowotny, Graz, 1961.

Codex Bodley contains tribal history. Edition A. Caso, Mexico, 1964.

Codex Boturini, in Mexico City, is part of a legendary history of the Mexica taking them from their ancestral home and into their long wanderings and sufferings.

Codex Cospiano, in the University Library, Bologna, is a tonalamatl also dealing with aspects of the planet Venus. Edition Duc de Loubat, Rome, 1898.

Codex Egerton (Codex Waecker Gotter), in the British Museum, is a Mixtec dynastic history. Edition C. A. Burland, Graz, 1965.

Codex Kingsborough (Petition of the Indians of Tepetlaoztoc), in the British Museum, covers conditions during the first years after the conquest. Edition Paso y Troncoso, Mexico, 1912.

Codex Laud, in the Bodleian Library at Oxford University, possibly dating to the tenth or eleventh century, is apparently Totonac calendrical material with information about the priesthood. It is dedicated to Tlaloc. Facsimile edition Akademische Druck-u. Verlaganstalt, Graz, 1966.

Codex Mendoza, in the Bodleian Library at Oxford University, is tribute lists of the Revered Speaker Moctezuma Xocoyotzin and a history of the Aztecs and their customs. Edition James Cooper Clark, London, 1938.

Codex Rios, in the Vatican Library, is a later missionary work on the Aztec cosmogony and calendar. Edition Duc de Loubat, Rome, 1901.

Codex Selden (Selden Roll) contains the Aztec migration legend. Edition C. A. Burland, Berlin, 1955.

Codex Telleriano-Remensis, in the Bibliotheque Nationale, Paris, contains history and theology with Spanish translation and notes. Edition E. T. Hamy, Paris, 1899.

Codex Vindobonensis (Vienna Codex), in the Nationalbibliothek, Vienna, is one of the books presented to Cortez before the fall of Mexico. It contains some Mixtec dynastic information, the creation story, the adventures of Quetzalcoatl, and a history the Toltec rulers of Tula. Facsimile edition Akademische Druck-u. Verlaganstalt, Graz, 1963.

III. For general information, the following are the sole three surviving Mayan codices.

Codex Dresdensis, held in Dresden, is a Mayan calendar for calculating astronomical ephemeris. Edition East German Publishing Houses, Berlin, 1964.

Codex Peresianus, held in Paris, contains material on the constellations of the Mayan zodiac. Edition Leon de Rosny, Paris, 1888.

Codex Tro-Cortesianus, held in Madrid, deals with Mayan agricultural rituals and hunting customs. Edition Junta de Relaciones Culturales, Madrid, 1930.

IV. There is a wealth of historical and scholarly literature on the Aztec world and particularly on the conquest of Mexico. The following are the principle works which provided information for this Tonalamatl.

Anderson, Arthur J. O., Rules of the Aztec Language. University of Utah Press, Salt Lake City UT, 1973.

Burland, C. A., The Gods of Mexico. G. P. Putnam's Sons, New York NY, 1967.

Keen, Benjamin, The Aztec Image in Western Thought. Rutgers University Press, New Brunswick NJ, 1971.

Sejourné, Laurette, Burning Water: Thought and Religion in Ancient Mexico. Shambhala, Berkeley CA, 1976.

Sejourné, Laurette, El Pensamiento Náhuatl Cifrado por los Calendarios. Siglo Veintiuno, Mexico DF, 1989.

Stuart, Gene S., The Mighty Aztecs. National Geographic Society, Washington DC, 1981.

Thompson, John Eric, Mexico Before Cortez. Scribners, New York/London, 1941.

Vaillant, George C., The Aztecs of Mexico. Penguin Books, 1975.

von Hagen, Victor Wolfgang, The Ancient Sun Kingdoms of the Americas. World Publishing Company, Cleveland/New York, 1961.

Waterman, T. T., The Delineation of the Day-Signs in the Aztec Manuscripts. University of California Publications in American Archaeology and Ethnology, Berkeley CA, Vol. 11, No. 6, 1916.

INDEX

A
Acatl, See Reed
Amatl (Paper), 9
Anahuac, 1
Astronomy, 30, 44
Atl, See Water
Azcapotzalco, 1
Aztlan, 1

B
Butterfly, 6, 8, 24, 42

C
Calendar Stone, 3-6, 10-**11**
Calli, See House
Calmecac, 4
Centeotl (God of Corn), 2, 38
Chalchiuhtlicue (Jade Skirt), *4*, 8, 10, 12, 14, 16, 22-**23**, 26, 46, 54
Chalchiuhtotolin (Jade Turkey), 6, 36, 46-**47**
Chalco, 1
Chantico (Goddess of the House), 6, 30, 48-**49**
Chicomecoatl (Seven Snake), 20, 26, 38
Chicomoztoc (Seven Caves), 1
Cholula, 16
Cihuateteo, 26, 34, 42, 50, 54
Cipactli, See Crocodile and Earth Monster
Citlallicue (Star Skirt), 14
Coatl, See Snake
Coatlicue (Snake Skirt), 12
Constellation, 2, 36
Copal (Incense), 24, 38
Copil, 12
Corn, 2, 26, 38
Cortes, 55
Coyolxauhqui (Golden Bells), 12, 24
Cozcacuauhtli, See Vulture
Crocodile, 2, **3**, 7, 14

Cuauhtemoc (Eagle Descending), 55
Cuauhtli, See Eagle
Cuciatl (Song), 50, 52
Cuetzpallin, See Lizard
Culhuacan, 1

D
Death, 2, **4**, 16, 24, 30, 32, 36, 38, 42, 44, 54-55
Deer, 2, **4**, 18, 50, 55
Dog, 2, **5**, 32, 40, 55-56

E
Eagle, 2, **6**, 7, 12, 40, 50, 55-56
Earth Monster, 3, 12, 14, 36, 38, 54
Earthquake, 2, **6**, 10, 16, 38, 56
Ehecatl (God of Wind), **3**, 8, 16

F
Fire, 5, 10, 12, 30, 48, 54
Flint, 2, **6**, 10, 12, 32, 42, 54
Flower, 2, **6**-8, 12, 16, 20, 38, 44, 50, 55-56

G
Grass, 2, **5**, 12, 28
Great Bear, 36
Guatemala, 1

H
House, 2, **4**, 7, 16, 42, 48, 54, 55-56
Huaxtec, 16
Huehuecoyotl (Old Coyote), 4, 20-**21**
Huehueteotl (Old God), 8, 30
Huitzilopochtli (Hummingbird of the South), 1, 12-**13**, 16, 32, 36, 54

I
Ilamacihuatl (Lady of Plenty), 14
Ilamatecuhtli (Lord of Plenty), 14
Itzacihuatl (Obsidian Lady), 42
Itzcoliuhqui (Obsidian Blade), 36

Itzcuintli, See Dog
Itzli (Knife), 52
Itzpapalotl (Obsidian Butterfly), 6, 8, 42-**43**, 54
Ixcoxcauhqui (He of the Yellow Face), 30
Ixcuina (Two-Faced), 38

J
Jaguar, 2, **5**, 7, 10, 16, 18, 34, 36, 55-56

L
Leap Years, 2, 55
Lizard, 2, **4**, 36

M
Macuiltochtli (Five Rabbit), 28, 36
Macuilxochitl (Five Flower), 44
Maguey, 28
Maize, 2, 38, 40
Malinalco, 12
Malinalli, See Grass
Malinalxochitl (Grass Flower), 12
Marigolds, 50
Matlalcueye (Blue Robe), 22
Maya, 1, 9, 16, 26, 55
Mayauel (Goddess of Pulque), 4, 28-**29**
Mazatl, See Deer
Medicine, 5, 34, 38
Merchants, 1, 30
Mercury, 44
Metl, 28
Metztli, 24
Mexi, 1
Mexica, 1, 12, 24, 28, 54
Mictlan (Land of the Dead), 5, 8, 14, 30, 32, 50, 56
Mictlantecuhtli (Lord of the Land of the Dead), 5, 14, 32-**33**
Miquiztli, See Death
Mixcoatl (Cloud Serpent), 2, 16
Mixtec, 1, 9

Moctezuma Xocoyotzin (Younger), 55
Monkey, 2, **5**, 10, 34
Montezuma, 4
Moon, 4, 8, 12, 24, 42

N
Nahuatl, 3, 9
Nemontemi (Nameless Days), 1, 2
Nezahualcoyotl (Fasting Coyote), 36
Numeral, 8

O
Ocelotl, See Jaguar
Octli, 28, 34
Ollin, See Earthquake
Olmec, 1
Omecihuatl (Lady of Two), 8, 14-**15**, 54
Omen, 9, 48, 54
Ometecuhtli (Lord of Two), 3, 12, 14, 54
Ozomatli, See Monkey

P
Palli, 54-56
Patecatl (God of Medicine), 5, 28, 34-**35**
Patolli (Board Game), 44
Piltzintecuhtli (Lord of the Planet Mercury), 44
Planet, 16, 44
Pleiades, 2, 44
Pochteca (Merchants), 30
Puebla, 16
Pulque, 4, 28, 34

Q
Quetzalcoatl (Plumed Serpent), 3, 8, 10, 16-**17**, 22, 26, 36, 44, 54-55
Quiahuitl, See Rain

R
Rabbit, 2, **4**, 18, 24, 28, 30, 34, 36, 52, 54, 56

Rain, 1-2, **4**, 6, 8, 10, 12, 22, 26, 40, 44, 55-56
Reed, 2, **5**, 7, 10, 12, 16, 22, 30, 38, 54

S
Sex, 4, 14, 20, 38, 44, 50
Snake, 2, **4**, 12, 20, 26, 30, 38, 55-56
Spaniards/Spanish, 9, 12, 16, 22, 38, 55
Star, 6, 14, 16, 30, 42, 44, 54
Sun, 1, 3, 8, 10, 12, 16, 18, 22, 24, 26, 34, 36, 44, 55-56

T
Tecciztecatl (God of the Moon), 4, 12, 24-**25**, 42
Tecpatl, See Flint
Telpochcalli, 4
Tenochtitlan (Place of the Cactus), 1, 12, 16, 55
Teocalli, 4
Teotihuacan, 1, 26
Tepeyollotl (Heart of the Mountain), 4, 18-**19**
Tepoztecatl (God of Drunkenness), 28
Texcoco, 1, 36
Tezcatlipoca (Smoking Mirror), 1, 3, 5, 8, 10, 12, 24, 34, 36-**37**, 40, 46, 54-55
Tlachtli (Ball Game), 52
Tlacopan, 1
Tlaelcuani (Filth Eater), 38
Tlahuizcalpantecuhtli (Lord of the House of the Dawn), 16
Tlaloc (Rain God), 1, 2, 4, 8, 10, 22, 26-**27**, 32, 44, 54
Tlalocs, 6, 26
Tlaltecuhtli (Lord of the Earth), 14
Tlaxcala, 22
Tlazolteotl (Goddess of Filth), 5, 8, 12, 30, 38-**39**
Tochtli, See Rabbit
Toltec, 1, 16, 36
Tonacacihuatl (Lady of Everything), 14
Tonacatecuhtli (Lord of Everything), 14

Tonalamatl (Book of Days), 9, 12, 14, 36
Tonalli (Days), 2-3, 7, 9-10
Tonalpohualli (Count of Days), 1, 7, 9, 55-56
Tonantzin (Earth Mother), 12, 38
Tonatiuh (Fifth Sun), 6, 8, 10-**11**, 16, 32
Totochtin (God of Drunkenness), 28
Tula, 1, 16, 36

U
Uixtocihuatl (Lady of Salt), 2

V
Venus, 16, 44
Vera Cruz, 1
Vulture, 2, **6**, 44

W
Water, 2, 4, **5**, 10, 22, 24, 46, 54, 56
Wind, 2-**3**, 7-8, 10, 16, 26, 48, 56

X
Xilonen (Goddess of Corn), 2, 26, 38
Xipe Totec (Flayed God), 6, 36, 40-**41**
Xiuhcoatl (Fire Serpent), 10
Xiuhtecuhtli (Lord of the Turquoise), 5, 8, 10, 30-**31**, 48, 52, 54
Xochimilco, 1
Xochipilli (Prince of Flowers), 5, 8, 44, 52-**53**, 55-56
Xochiquetzal (Flower Feather), 6, 8, 18, 38, 44, 50-**51**-52, 54-56
Xochitl, See Flower
Xolotl (Evening Star), 6, 16, 44-**45**, 54

Y
Yacatecuhtli (God of Merchants), 30
Yaotl (God of Darkness), 36
Year-bearers, 54-55
Yucatan, 1, 9

Z
Zapotecs, 1